CHILDHOOD,

WAR

AND

PEACE

To: Pat Brennan

Mulholland

Biography of Len Mulholland

Note for Librarians: A cataloguing record for this book is available from Library and Archives Canada at www.collectionscanada.ca/amicus/index-e.html
ISBN 1-4120-7320-0

Printed in Victoria, BC, Canada. Printed on paper with minimum 30% recycled fibre. Trafford's print shop runs on "green energy" from solar, wind and other environmentally-friendly power sources.

PUBLISHING

Offices in Canada, USA, Ireland and UK
This book was published *on-demand* in cooperation with Trafford Publishing. On-demand publishing is a unique process and service of making a book available for retail sale to the public taking advantage of on-demand manufacturing and Internet marketing. On-demand publishing includes promotions, retail sales, manufacturing, order fulfilment, accounting and collecting royalties on behalf of the author.

Book sales for North America and international:
Trafford Publishing, 6E–2333 Government St.,
Victoria, BC v8t 4p4 CANADA
phone 250 383 6864 (toll-free 1 888 232 4444)
fax 250 383 6804; email to orders@trafford.com
Book sales in Europe:
Trafford Publishing (uk) Limited, 9 Park End Street, 2nd Floor
Oxford, UK ox1 1hh UNITED KINGDOM
phone 44 (0)1865 722 113 (local rate 0845 230 9601)
facsimile 44 (0)1865 722 868; info.uk@trafford.com
Order online at:
trafford.com/05-2215

10 9 8 7 6 5 4 3 2 1

ACKNOWLEDGEMENTS.

First and most important I would like to acknowledge the support of my wife, Anna. In the years since the end of the war we have shared the adventure of life together. She has listened to my stories and supported my effort to record those years of my childhood, my war experiences and most significantly building a new life together after the war. In the last few months especially I appreciated her patience and for tolerating my neglect of the yard.

In writing this book I would like to thank Betty Stafford Smith, Ph.D. for her encouragement without which this biography might never have been written. Also for the many hours and patience editing and re-editing the manuscript until she was satisfied that it was right. I cannot thank you enough Betty!

I also want to thank John Welsted, Ph.D, for his valued contribution in reading the whole manuscript, and specifically in enabling me to provide a clear description of the code system that was used by special agents.

FORWORD.

I started writing my story because a book was written about me published in 1980, ('Night Drop at Ede' by John Windsor). When I finally read this book about three years later, I was quite disturbed to find that it was not actually the true story of my experiences. By the early nineties this started to bother me enough that I decided to write my own true story. I also decided that it would be interesting to describe my early years in the Dutch East Indies to allow the reader to see how events unfolded. I arrived in Holland the day World War II was declared - an eager young man just out of high school, and was overtaken by world events. I have also covered the immediate postwar years to show how my war experience affected my whole life path.

TABLE OF CONTENTS:

Chapter Twelve
Living and Working in Germany and Sabotage: 1944-1945

PART IV:
Chapter Thirteen
Germany Surrenders, back to England, and Getting Married: 1945
Chapter Fourteen
Sri Lanka with Force 136 (Covert Espionage and Sabotage)
Chapter Fifteen
Atom Bomb ends War, a Strange Offer and a Wedding in Colombo
Chapter Sixteen
Going Home, Getting Divorced and Re-connecting with Normal Life
Chapter Seventeen
Finding a Job and Meeting Anna, receiving the Order of the Bronze Lion from Queen Wilhelmina
Chapter Eighteen
Proposing to Anna, Receiving the M.C. and Getting Married
Chapter Nineteen
Three Years in New Guinea: 1947-1950

Postscript – A New Life in Canada

One-Time-Pad code

The 'Silk' Figure 1

INTRODUCTION

September 20, 1920, was the day I was born; in Surabaya on the island of Java in what was then the Dutch East Indies, the present day Indonesia. I spent the first eighteen years of my life on Java and have fond memories of my carefree and easy youth when nothing seemed to matter and having fun was more important than anything else. My recollection of my early years is probably not complete nor in chronological order. An old man's memories of his life as a child or even as an adult can never be an accurate account of the facts. But it is the way I remember the events or perhaps the way I would like to remember them without consciously trying to paint them in a better light. For the war years I did not want to rely solely on my memory and managed to obtain a huge number of documents from war archives in The Hague and in London. I have made extensive use of these documents to keep the order of events in the proper sequence. When I think back on the past I mostly remember the pleasant things in my life while the unpleasant parts have faded with time. I find it hard to recall the bad events except those in my very early years during the marriage break-up of my parents, but I know I cannot assume that all the following years were smooth sailing.

PART 1
Chapter One
Growing up in the Dutch East Indies: 1920-1939

My earliest recollection of any significance was probably when I was about six years old. At that time we lived on a sugar plantation about twenty miles from Surabaya, in the eastern part of Java where I was born and where my Dad was an engineer in the refinery. I remember that I spent a lot of time playing with my Meccano set.

My life as a young boy involved going to school by bus to the nearest town; each plantation had its own bus. School was from seven to twelve, five days a week; Saturday was half a day. School for me has always been fun, especially in those days. I loved to meet new friends from the surrounding refineries who all went to the same school. The five-mile ride on the bus was always exciting: we played games, teased the girls, and did all the things little boys do and perhaps shouldn't do! Of course, we got into mischief once in a while and if caught we would end up in the principal's office. Each new teacher was a new challenge. I remember that one of the boys would bring a snake into the classroom and release it during classes. It was a totally harmless snake and, if left alone, would soon have left the room, which was wide open on one side. But it always caused quite a bit of consternation. He would repeat this stunt every time we got a new teacher.

The Brantas River was about a quarter of a mile from the plantation. At the end of the dry season it was about a hundred meters wide, but it became a raging, ominous, fast flowing body of water twice as wide during the monsoon, occasionally overflowing its banks. I loved going to the river with my fishing rod which consisted of a bamboo pole, a piece of string and a hook made out of a bent pin. One of my pockets would be full of worms that sometimes I would forget to remove before depositing my shorts in the laundry hamper!

I would walk along the riverbank, barefoot of course; naturally, my shoes always came off as soon as we came home from school. Often I would just sit in the shade of a tree with my hook and worm dangling in the water, listening to the sounds of the birds and whiling away the hot afternoons. I would usually catch a fish or two: small muddy creatures that were not edible and always thrown back in the water. The banks were steep and about five feet high during the dry season. A wide muddy strip separated the bank from the water. As there were lots of crocodiles, it was better to stay on the high bank rather than to walk on the muddy strip. A crocodile would have an unfair advantage over a boy into heavy mud above his ankles.

I do recall that things were not going well at home. My dad would often raise his voice at my mum because something had made him angry. I could never understand why he was angry and as far as I was concerned, there was nothing that my mother did that could make him so angry. When I asked him a question the answer always seemed to be a stern "NO". As time went on I became very resentful of him. Maybe he sensed this because I gradually became the co-recipient of his angry outbursts, often for no reason that I could understand.

Many years later when my sons were growing up, I reflected on this early period of my life. I realized that I too, was easily inclined to brush them off with a "No," especially after I had just come home from a day's work and wanted some time to relax. I decided that from then on I would only give them my answer after I had given what they had to say some serious consideration. It was quite amazing how it also changed the boys' behaviour; they seemed to realize that they had to prepare their questions properly if they wanted to receive serious consideration.

I remember it was sugar-harvesting time and the refinery was operating around the clock. My dad was away a lot because of some mechanical problems at the refinery and only came home for a few hours to sleep. One morning, just after he came home, there was a violent outbreak between my mum and dad and a lot of angry words were spoken. That evening, after my dad had left for the plant, my mother called my sister and me over and motioned us to sit down in front of her. She looked at us for quite a while without saying a word, then drew a deep breath and said, "Your mommy does not want to stay with daddy anymore and I am going away to-morrow. You can come with me if you want to, but if you want to stay with daddy that is OK too". It didn't take me long to decide: she had barely finished talking when I said, "I want to come with you." My little sister started to cry; of course she wanted my mum to stay, but she finally decided that she wanted to stay with her daddy. She had always been a daddy's girl and my dad was always nice to her. That night, after my sister was put to bed, my mum sat down next to me and told me that we were going to leave the next morning to catch the train to Semarang on the north coast of central Java, some two hundred kilometres to the west of where we were living. She told me to pack my toys and my clothes and go to bed; our train was leaving shortly after six and we had to get up very early.

The next morning we left; I was six, maybe seven years old. We were going to stay with my aunt Tonnie, my mom's sister, and Uncle Hank. Tonnie was short for Antoinette but nobody ever called her that. She was my favourite aunt, always full of fun. My past life and my Dad faded from my memory very quickly; I was happy that I no longer had to endure my Dad's angry outbursts. Life was so different at my new home; my uncle never raised his voice and always seemed to have a friendly word to say.

There were some geese in the backyard, to keep the snakes away; they were also very good watchdogs. I was warned that I should be very careful playing too close to them because they could bite. I was scared of them especially when they put their heads close to the ground and come towards me making an angry hissing sound. One day I was sitting on the swing and having a great time. Suddenly I felt a terrible pain my back. One of the geese was swinging with me while holding on to my seat! My uncle came running laughing to the rescue; he grabbed the goose by its neck and pulled him off me. I jumped off the swing and ran inside to look at my backside in the mirror. I saw a nasty big bruise; it was mighty sore, and for the next two weeks I was only able to sit with all my weight on one side.

We stayed with my uncle and aunt for just over a year. One day a friend of my uncle arrived and he stayed for a few days. He was a very jovial sort and seemed to laugh a lot and I liked him. I noticed that my Mom liked him also which somehow made me rather happy. About a month after his visit my mother decided that we were moving to a small place, called Tegal about one hundred kilometres further west. She rented a small bungalow where we lived for the next two years. I noticed that my Mom received an incredible number of letters. Later I found out they all came from the same man who had visited my aunt and uncle. He was the administrator of a sugar plantation and refinery some twenty kilometres out of town. Two years later my Mom married him and he became my stepfather; I quickly considered him as my real and only father. He was a wonderful person and we became very close and the best of friends. His own children had gone to Holland with their mother and I do not think that he ever heard much from them other than the usual birthday and season's greetings.

We now lived on a plantation where there was no school bus service; consequently all the kids who lived there had to board somewhere near their school. I was able to stay with my grandparents in Bandung about three hundred kilometres away to attend school and I only went home during the holidays. My natural grandmother had passed away and my grandfather had remarried and had two children, my uncles, both younger than me by two and three years. They would often tease me by saying that I address them properly as uncle before their first name. I usually replied that I would give both of them a licking before I'd ever do that!

Going home for the holidays was quite an event because I had to change trains; at this time I was eight years old. My grandmother would attach a big cardboard sign to me securely held by strings around my neck and around my torso, tied firmly to make sure that I wouldn't get lost during the four hour train trip. On the sign was my name, the place where I had to change trains, my final destination and a phone number to call if I should run into problems. Of course there were numerous older people, ladies in particular, who took pity on me, or perhaps just wanted to take care of me and they showered me with all kinds of goodies, lemonade, sandwiches, etc. I had my own sandwiches but they insisted that I eat theirs and I gladly obliged. I was very popular and there was no possible way that I would I ever have ended up on the wrong train; they all made sure of that!

The holidays were spent mainly on the tennis court and in the swimming pool. We played tennis from dawn to about eight a.m. when it became too hot on the court; then home for a quick snack; swimming in the pool till noon; home for dinner, back to the pool till five; home for a sandwich and then to the tennis court again till nine. The adults usually played tennis in the evenings so we had to be the ball boys. However, in between games we would hit the ball back and forth. Sometimes there would be only three adults and then they would often ask me to make up the four.

After one year with my grandparents, I was able to board with the principal of the school in Tegal, only twenty kilometres from the refinery. So I was now able to come home not only during vacations but on weekends too. I liked being home, but these weekends were often rather boring since none of the other kids were home to play with. In town I at least had my classmates.

I cannot recall anything of significance during the next few years except for the fact that this was the period when I had my first experience with the sea. The people I stayed with during the week were friends of the harbour master who would frequently come over for a chat. One day he asked me whether I would be interested in going with him some weekend to a ship that was at anchor about three miles offshore. There were always ships at anchor offshore waiting to be loaded or unloaded into barges. Whenever a ship arrived, the harbour master had to go out on a motor launch to get the details of what had to be loaded or unloaded and then arrange for the barges to be towed out. However, most of the time the barges were dispatched as soon as word came that a ship had arrived. After that first trip out to the ships, I was hooked and tried to go at every opportunity afterwards. If I was there during lunch hour, which often happened, the officers usually invited me to the dining room to have lunch with them. I loved to be out on the ocean to watch what was going on and usually went back to shore with one of the tugboats when they towed the barges back. I think it was those great experiences that influenced me, before I finished high school, to decide to spend the rest of my life at sea.

The next big change in my life came when I went to high school. It was 1932, the recession was in full swing and scores of people were laid off work. Most people went back to Holland. My dad, as I now viewed my stepfather, was retired early with a very meagre pension, a fraction of what it would have been if he had been able to work until it was his time to retire. He decided to move into town and start his own business. The closest high school was in Bandung and my parents could not afford board and room for me. However they managed to get me into a boarding house for orphans run by the Salvation Army. I was there for one year and this was without doubt the unhappiest episode of my life. I had nothing in common with the other kids, since I was the only one attending high school while others of my age were going to trade school. We slept in dormitories; every morning someone would come in to wake us up by clapping his hands. We had to say grace before every meal and go to church every Sunday. These church services seemed endless and I found them extremely boring. This was also my worst school year academically and I barely passed my exams. There was one pleasant memory of this period: I joined the Boy Scouts that I really enjoyed and it was a welcome change from the atmosphere in the boarding house too. On weekends we would go out quite often for camping trips. What a treat that was! I would not have missed those trips for anything in the world.

Fortunately by the end of my school year my dad's business was going very well so that the following year he could afford to board me with a family in Bandung. What a relief to have left the Salvation Army boarding house! After that year I had to work very hard to catch up to the other kids. The teachers knew my situation and helped me with extra lessons and some tutoring.

At the end of my second year at school in Bandung my parents decided that I should go to the high school in Djakarta, my mother arranged for me to stay with my real father who lived in a small city some sixty kilometres south of Djakarta. He had remarried to a woman who had a daughter by her first marriage.

My stepmother and her daughter they were both very friendly and we got along fine. It seemed at first that my father had found the happiness that he never had with my mother. Sadly, he soon took every opportunity to tell me, very subtly at first, but then viciously, what a bad person my mother was. I adored my mother and told him on several occasions that I would rather not have him talk about my mother at all. As far as I was concerned she had done nothing wrong. But he didn't stop until one day, when he was saying particularly nasty things about my mum, something suddenly snapped inside me. Everything went blank; I picked up a dining room chair and was going to hit him over the head with it when a loud scream brought me to my senses. My stepmother had walked in and seeing the expression on my face had let out the scream. I realized what I had been about to do in a blind fit of rage. I also realized that I could have killed him; without saying another word I went to my room, packed all my belongings and left. That was the last time I saw my father. I went to a friend and asked his parents if I could stay with them till the end of the school year. I told them what had happened and that I had no intention of going back home, ever. They were good enough to let me stay. I phoned my mother and told her what had happened and where I was. My mother talked to my friend's mother and it was agreed that I could stay with them as long as necessary. It has been difficult for me to relate this episode of my life and now, almost seventy years later, I still think about the fact that I had come to within a whisker of killing my own father.

I had to commute to school in Djakarta by electric train that left at 6 a.m. sharp. The trip took about forty-five minutes that left me fifteen minutes to walk to my school. I had to walk fast to just make it on time, but, if the train was a few minutes late, I was late. When this happened to any of us, rather than walk to the classroom we went straight to the principal's office to report that the train had arrived late.

The train trips were a lot of fun. As soon as we boarded, out came the cards and we would start to play bridge. Fast bridge, no time for talking! The next dealer would deal the next deck while the first play was still on to minimize the delay between plays. We often played very unconventionally; for instance, each of us in turn playing three no trump, regardless of the hand we were dealt and without bidding. Those of you who are familiar with bridge will easily understand the crazy results of these utterly wild games. But we had fun and sometimes stayed on after the train had arrived at the station to finish the hand, sometimes long enough for the train to start the return trip! It then became a mad scramble to bail out before it was too late because those electric trains gained speed very fast. On the way home in the afternoon we played different games. One of these was a contest to be the last one to board the train. This contest meant running alongside the back of the last car as long as possible before jumping on. The challenge was that the platform came to a sudden end and if you didn't get on board before the train was going too fast, or before you reached the end of the platform, you were out of luck and watched the train disappear in the distance! This meant a two-hour wait before the next train, and it was a boring train ride without all your schoolmates.

After one year my parents decided that I should move to Djakarta. They made arrangements with another aunt of mine who agreed that I could stay with her for a year. The extra room in the house was already occupied by 'Oma', my other grandmother, so they redecorated the detached garage for me and made it into a very comfortable place. I loved it because it gave me a lot of freedom and allowed me to do things that I would not have been able to do if my room had been in the house, for instance sneaking out to go to a party on Saturday night after the others in the house had gone to bed. I remember coming home just after daylight at six, walking past the kitchen window when my grandmother saw me and I remember her shaking her finger at me and smiling at the same time! She never told anyone else, the sweet soul, and it remained a secret between us forever.

My mother moved to Djakarta towards the end of this school year, and became the supervisor of a large boarding house for girls, mostly orphaned teens. She decided that I should move to a private 'boarding house', for lack of a better word, for boys. These boarding houses were quite large and were necessary because high schools were only located in the larger cities. My boarding house consisted of three dormitory buildings, each with accommodation for a 'house master' and his family, and a large dining and kitchen facility. Many parents sent their children to Holland when they reached high school age but those that preferred to have their children closer would send them to the cities to stay at these boarding houses. Many of the boys were from very wealthy parents and often had their own car or motorcycle. I remember that one boy had a Harley Davidson and he was quite the envy of us all! This school year was a fun year, as was the one before. My parents would quite often get a letter from the housemaster to tell them that I had been a "bad boy". I think that I should have been in big trouble, but because I was the top of the class I usually escaped with a reprimand.

I have fond memories of those last two years of high school. However it was time for me to become serious and think of my future after high school. I had decided that I wanted to spend the rest of my life at sea and go to naval college in Amsterdam. My mother was very happy with my decision because it was well known that this particular college maintained a very strict discipline like any military college. If I were aware of this it would not have made a particle of difference. All I could think about was going overseas, being on my own and going to a new and very different school that would prepare me for life at sea.

My application to naval college was submitted and about the middle of August, 1939 the letter of acceptance came with the message that I was to report to the school at the beginning of September. The only boat available at that time was a Japanese freighter with some passenger accommodation. The boat was already in the harbour and supposed to leave in one or two days. We booked my passage and the next day, after a tearful farewell (on my mother's part) I was on board, with two large suitcases and my bicycle. It was almost seven years before I saw my mother again.

I was very excited to be leaving the Dutch East Indies and going to Holland, just by myself, and going to the naval college. The passenger accommodation on the ship was very mediocre; the place needed a good scrub and a paint job. But...at that age, eighteen, who cares! There was an attempt to prepare western food for the passengers, including a large group of missionaries. The missionaries had been in China for many years and were now going back to their homeland, Belgium, for a few months to see their relatives for one last time before returning to China for good. I often wondered if they were ever able to get back, but I suspect that they all remained in Belgium for the duration of the war and perhaps never did return to China. The political situation in China had changed dramatically after the war and I doubt that the revolutionary government in China would have allowed missionaries into the country.

During the trip I spent many hours on deck with one of the oldest missionaries who had been in China for more than thirty years. He told me that he could speak several Chinese languages fluently (I say languages rather than dialects because he told me that the people speaking one language could not understand someone speaking another). He would keep me spellbound with his stories about life in China, and the addiction of Chinese people to opium. In many areas the growing of opium poppies was the main source of income. Addiction was rampant. If there is one thing that Mao Tse Tung accomplished after the war, it was that he made China practically opium free.

The days flew by; we were in Singapore for one day and night, then in Colombo in Sri Lanka for a day. We were steaming through the Red Sea, within a few miles of the eastern entrance of the Suez Canal, when there was suddenly a lot of excitement among the Japanese crew. The boat was hastily decorated with all the flags they could find and the crew changed into clean white uniforms. As passengers we had no idea what was going on but, about an hour later, when we were in the Suez Canal, about to meet another boat going in the opposite direction, we found out the reason for all this activity. The other boat was German and as they passed, the crews of both ships were lined up at the railings waving flags at each other while both ships blew their horns. It was quite puzzling none of the passengers had any idea why there was such a display of friendship between these two nations.

Most of the passengers disembarked in Marseilles and continued to their final destinations by train. The train station was in turmoil but, as I had never been to Europe before, I didn't think anything of it. All I remember of the trip between Marseilles and Paris is finding out that France had declared war on Germany. Paris was in total chaos, but I found out that the last train north to Amsterdam would leave in about four hours. The trains from the south of France arrive at the Gare du Lyon and the trains going to the north leave from the Gare du Nord. Normally, one would just step onto a connecting train to go to the other station, but this day there was none. All the available trains were readied to take army personnel to the eastern front and all the platforms were jammed with soldiers and their wives or sweethearts saying good bye. It was an emotional sight to see many of them clutched in an embrace for a long time and scarcely speaking a word.

While on the train to Amsterdam, I learned that England had also declared war on Germany. When I finally arrived at the college, about a week late, I was told that my mother had called several times. One of the first things I did was to send her a telegram, no e-mails then, to let her know that all was well.

Chapter 2
First Year of College: 1939-1940

College was a new and different experience for me: the school, the discipline and my classmates, who were mostly born and raised in Holland. They talked about politics, a subject that was totally foreign to me. I liked the subjects taught at the college since most of them were of a technical nature and based on some form of mathematics. Math had been my favourite subject throughout high school. The only rather boring subject was geography since it dealt only with coastal cities and towns, islands and waterways. A typical geography test, for instance, was: "travel along the coast from Halifax south and around Florida to Houston and name all the cities, river mouths, prominent features, etc. you pass. Another example would be: "from Amsterdam along the coast through the Straight of Gibraltar, along the European coast to the mouth of the Suez Canal, etc".

We were only allowed outside the compound Wednesdays, Saturdays and Sundays from two until ten p.m. If you were caught doing anything you were not supposed to, this privilege was denied. For me, this meant that I didn't get to see the outside world for the first two months or so! I was a smoker and smoking was strictly prohibited anywhere inside the compound. We were constantly being watched by 'boatsmen', who were something like sergeant majors in the army. There was one boatsman for approximately thirty students. They had been around for quite a while and knew exactly when and where to look and knew every trick you could possibly think of. They seemed to come from nowhere when you least expected them and before you knew it you had a ticket. If you got caught smoking it meant 'two days arrest'. If it happened between Sunday and Wednesday it meant that you had to stay in on Wednesday and again the following Saturday. And if you got caught again before your arrest was up, the punishment just kept accumulating. Staying in did not mean that you could lie down and sleep or do anything else unproductive. The standard weekend job was washing the linoleum floors of the classrooms, the dining room and the dormitories as well as the concrete stairways and the dormitories. Also included was at least two hours of study in the classroom, all of this under the watchful eye of one of the boatsmen.

When I finally did get out of the main gate during the first part of November, I took the train to Rotterdam where my guardian lived. Every student who did not have his parents in Holland had to have a guardian. My parents knew this man but I had never met him. He had a son about my age who soon introduced me to his group of friends and neighbours. This particular area where they lived was on the very outskirts of Rotterdam in between two small lakes. My guardian had a sailboat that his son used most of the time and when I went with him I met other people. This was definitely better than washing floors and I realized what I had missed all this time. From now on I was going to toe the line at college, or, at least, to try to not get caught smoking again. It was November and soon all boating on the lakes would come to an end. In my case, I was not too successful at not getting caught and for the next three weeks I was washing floors again!

However, maybe all this staying in and spending extra time studying was good for me after all, because I was the top of my class. As was getting my report card, my guardian would receive a letter from the college to tell him about my bad behaviour. When I knew that he was going to confront me with this letter, I always made sure that I had my report card with me to show him. This usually did the trick: if my marks were that good, I couldn't possibly be that bad!

The war raged on and the news was not good. Somehow everybody felt that Holland would stay neutral again, as had happened before in World War I, and nobody seemed overly concerned. As the winter months approached, the days became shorter and, as I was used to sunrise and sundown always at six o'clock in Indonesia, this was a new experience. All students went home for Christmas, my first one in Holland, also my first experience with snow. Getting acquainted with life in Holland was fun, getting to know Dutch girls was also fun and so was throwing snowballs at them.

PART II

Chapter Three
THE GERMAN INVASION, GRADUATION, A LAST
CAREFREE SUMMER: 1940

Life changed dramatically on May 10, 1940.
Very early in the morning, probably around 5 a.m., I
was woken up to the sound of voices and strange
noises in the distance like explosions. I tried to get back
to sleep because I knew that it was too early to get up,
but the voices were getting louder and very excited
and I finally was aware that half the dormitory was at
the windows and getting increasingly agitated. Shortly
after one of the officers came into the dormitory. He
told us that the German army had invaded Holland
and that we were to get dressed as soon as possible
and assemble in the dining room for breakfast and to
get further instructions.

A hush fell over the dormitory and everybody
hurried to get washed and dressed. In the dining room
the mood was very subdued. All of us were wondering
what would happen next and anticipating the
instructions we were going to receive. As we were
having breakfast, the commandant and first officer
came into the dining room and told us that school
would be suspended until further notice; we were to
change into dress uniform, pack our personal
belongings and go home. The college would get in
touch with us to let us know when classes were to
resume.

My friend Gert, with whom I had spent a few
weekends in the past, and who had a motorcycle,
asked me if I wanted to ride with him and spend a few

days at his parents. I gratefully accepted his invitation and about an hour later we were on our way to Voorburg, just east of The Hague and about fifteen kilometres north of Rotterdam. Gert's parents welcomed us, and yes, of course I could stay with them as long as I wanted. I was very happy to accept their offer because Gert was a very good friend and we got along well. We listened to the news broadcasts, trying to make some sense of an extremely chaotic situation. There were appeals for volunteers from the home guard, the hospitals, fire departments and many more. That first afternoon we decided to go to the home guard to see if they could use our services. We were issued with an identification armband and given the job of patrolling the streets in a four-block area from 8p.m. to 8a.m. and to report anything suspicious or unusual. So that is what we did for the next four nights; nothing happened but at least it made us feel useful.

The Germans had advanced through Holland with a bit of resistance here and there, but our forces were no match for them. On the fourth day we saw large columns of smoke billowing in the southern sky and heard that Rotterdam had been bombed. I was seething with anger and could not understand why they would ever bomb a defenceless city. I heard later that it was because they had met fierce resistance at the main bridge at the southern end of the city. Holland surrendered and so ended the war that had lasted only four days.

Since most of the people I knew lived in and close to Rotterdam, I decided to go there and Gert offered to take me on his motorbike. I thanked his parents for their hospitality and we were on our way.

The main road was packed with scores of people, on bikes and on foot pulling carts behind them loaded with some of their belongings leaving Rotterdam. They all had horror stories to tell about the bombing. The bombs had fallen mainly in the centre of the city and the outlying areas were not damaged. Since this was where most of my friends lived, we kept going. Closer to Rotterdam we started to smell the smoke and the flow of people going in the opposite direction grew as we came closer to our destination. Hardly anyone spoke and the expression on their faces was a combination of disbelief, anger and disgust.

My friends in Hillegersberg, a suburb of Rotterdam, were all fine. The days following my arrival in Rotterdam are a blur. The Germans immediately confiscated several government buildings for their headquarters and hotels to house the men. They were soon to be seen all over the city. They kept pretty well to themselves and it was obvious that they were trying their best to be nice to the Dutch people only to be met, in return, by a polite and very reserved response. As far as my friends and I were concerned the war was not over; it had just begun. Gradually the realization set in that Hitler had overrun our country with brute force and with hardly any resistance. Did they expect us to be friendly to them and accept them just as the Austrians had done before? Our discussions from that moment on were mainly cantered on what we could do to help the Allies. There were lots of suggestions, most of them very impractical but, if nothing else, it made us feel good.

Then I heard from the college that classes were to resume on the following Monday and I boarded the train back to Amsterdam. I was now looking forward to the summer holidays that were only a few weeks away. Back in college, the talk was all about the German occupation and, strangely enough we all thought that the war would be over in a few months, with a victory for the Allies of course. I have no idea on what we based our estimate of the duration of the war, but everybody seemed to think that way. We had no knowledge of the unprepared condition of the British forces, but we knew that the British Navy was certainly superior to the German navy. We were also unaware of the fact that the Germans had a large number of submarines.

That summer our holidays were mainly spent on and near the water. It was a welcome change from life at college and oddly separate from the war. We listened on the radio to news from London about the war. We had to be careful since it was forbidden to listen to any radio stations other than the German and the local ones. That summer also became our first experience with the blackout. It was not easy to ensure that no light was showing on the outside. The streets were regularly patrolled and if a glimpse of light was detected you soon had somebody ringing the doorbell to draw your attention to it. In the beginning they were pretty lenient but after a few weeks warning tickets were issued and a second offence meant a stiff penalty. Negotiating our way on dark nights became a very new experience for all of us. Later that year, on a weekend at home, I ran smack into a steel telephone pole. I passed out and fell so that my back hit the edge of the sidewalk. I came to a while later with a mighty sore back and a very swollen and sore nose.

The summer vacation came to an end and I went back to college.

Much to our surprise we realized that there were five or six cadets at college who were German sympathizers. It was hard to believe and as far as most of us were concerned totally unacceptable. The other cadets treated them as traitors with increasing hostility. I couldn't stand the sight of any of them but I detested one cadet in particular. I would give him a shoulder whenever possible as we walked past each other in the hallway and on one occasion this led to blows between us. Normally a fight would result in a two-day arrest for both of us but on this occasion I was told to report to the commandant. I stood at attention in front of the commandant's desk. He looked at me for a long time and then said: "I realize and understand why you did this but I want you to understand that the college is under scrutiny by the German occupation forces and that we are under orders to report incidents such as these. Let me warn you that if there is a repeat I will have to expel you from the college. "Is that understood?" "Yes sir". He looked at me for a while and then a smile came on his face and said: "I think that I would have done the same thing and now get out of my office!"

I took the commandant's warning to heart and tried to ignore the individual for the next few months. He knew that I had been called on the carpet and each time he saw me looking at him, he had a smirk on his face. I learned later that he had reported me to the Dutch Nazi Party and they in turn had phoned the commandant to give me a warning. But the standoff came to an abrupt end when he purposely shouldered me in the hall as we passed each other. I looked back and when I saw the triumphant smile on his face, I could not contain myself and planted my fist in it. The other cadets immediately grabbed us to prevent us from further fighting. A short time later the commandant called me on the carpet again. He was very conciliatory. Apparently, one of the boatsmen had witnessed the incident and had reported to him that I had been provoked. Nevertheless he said that he had no choice but to expel me from residence but that I could keep attending the college. I learned later that he reported to the German authorities that he had suspended me and had taken it upon himself to allow me to continue to attend classes so that I could write my final exams.

My friend Gert had been attending college but boarding out since the German invasion. Gert had chosen not to continue as an intern; he had rented a suite in an attic consisting of a large living room with a coke-fired, potbellied stove and a fairly large bedroom. He immediately invited me to come to live with him, an invitation I eagerly accepted and I moved in with him a few days later. The end of the year was about five months away, and I was glad to be moving out and no longer enduring the constraints of the college. It was a treat to go home after school and be free to do as I wished. The suite was in the attic of a huge house bordering on a park and was owned by a lady named Mimi, who lived on the fourth floor directly below us. She told us right away to call her by her first name that made us feel very comfortable. The house was within half a block of a bus stop. We had to make our own meals and always went home at weekends. When we returned we usually brought a suitcase full of prepared dinners that we only had to warm up on top of the stove. Since we did not own a fridge, we stored our food in a box on a ledge outside our bedroom window.

We got along very well with Mimi who would invite us down for dinner or for an evening of listening to classical music. She was also a fan of the theatre and often managed to get a couple of extra tickets for us, which was great. She obviously liked us very much and after a while more or less took 'her boys' under her wing. It was bitterly cold that winter and during the evening we had the stove red-hot. Our bedroom was not heated; despite this we kept our window wide open. My bed was in front of the window while Gert's was against the opposite wall. He had a sleeping bag and I slept under four or five blankets and this way we both managed to keep warm. However, one morning I woke up with about five inches of snow on top of my blanket at the foot of the bed. Fortunately it was dry snow, so I was able to carry the snow on the blanket to the window and dump it outside.

At the end of our school year, after we had written our final exams, we had our year-end ball. We had been planning several months ahead for this occasion. It was always a 'by invitation only' affair restricted to parents, guardians, and lady friends of the cadets. One of the cadets came up with the idea of inviting a couple of prostitutes to the ball and approached me with his plan. Since I was not an intern, he suggested that I try to find a couple of women in the red-light district who were willing to go to the ball for a sum of money that we could afford to pay. So Gert and I found a couple of 'ladies' who were willing to do what we wanted. We told them that they were to go to the college on the night of the ball, come in with the other invited guests, and act as if they were also invited. They were to sit down at one of the unreserved tables, behave properly, and under no circumstances to show any recognition if they saw us. When the music and dancing started they could let themselves go and invite one of the older uniformed men with gold stripes on his sleeves; that is the officers, not the cadets. We paid them the agreed price and left.

Only the three of us knew anything about the plan. On the night of the ball, when most of the cadets and several of the invited guests had arrived, we spotted the two women. They were easy to identify because of their tight, short dresses and the excess of make-up on their faces; apart from that the two girls did as we had asked, behaved very correctly, and sat down at one of the tables. We noticed that some of the officers were talking to each other with sideway glances at the women, obviously wondering who had invited them, or perhaps whether they had been invited at all. We sat innocently at a table on the opposite side of the ballroom from where we could watch the proceedings. It transpired just as we had hoped; as soon as the music started the 'ladies' both got up and asked a couple of officers to dance. This was highly unusual, as it was customary for officers to dance the first dance with the special guests. As the officers were not 'ballroom dancers' this also made the officers feel even more awkward and uncomfortable. The 'ladies' went on to dance with some of the cadets and even they were obviously ill at ease. We could barely keep a straight face and finally had to remove ourselves from the scene so that we could laugh to our heart's content without anybody seeing us. The prostitutes left after a couple of hours and we never saw them again. We sure had our money's worth of fun! The officers and cadets never found out who the 'ladies' were, where they came from and who had invited them, but it was very obvious that they did not belong at the dance.

After the ball Gert and I went bar-hopping for a while and when we came home in the early hours of the morning, feeling no pain, we went up the stairs singing and banging on the walls and waking up every person in the house. Late the next morning Mimi called us down and when we entered her room she burst out laughing. "I heard you come home last night"', she said, "and you certainly were very noisy". Every household in the building had called her to complain about her noisy tenants. I begged that we should be forgiven since it was our farewell to the college and we would soon leave for good. We said our good-byes and thanked her for taking such good care of us. Gert left on his motorcycle for Voorburg, and I took the train to Rotterdam.

I began to realize that attending college, and studying for final exams, I had been unaware of what was happening in the rest of the country. I discovered that numerous resistance groups had been, or were in the process of being, formed. These groups were mainly involved in the distribution of leaflets produced by the underground press and in obtaining food distribution coupons for Jewish families. By this time all the Jews had to wear a big yellow star on their chest and were harassed at every opportunity by German soldiers and by members of the Dutch 'National Socialist Party'. Since the coupon distribution offices were mostly staffed, or at least overseen by members of this party, most of the Jews were quite uncomfortable picking up their ration coupons. The many coupons that found their way to the underground were distributed to Jewish families, so that they did not have to go to the office to pick them up. Jewish houses were under constant surveillance during the day, so the delivery had to be done after dark during the night.

There was a lot of talk about sabotage. In fact, it was already taking place by the workers in the factories and by employees who worked in the offices that produced identification cards. Soon after the occupation we were all issued identification cards that included our photograph and fingerprints. A lot of blank ID cards found their way to the underground and these were mainly issued to underground workers or to anyone whose real name was, or could possibly be, on a list kept by the German Gestapo. Our minds were increasingly occupied by what we could do in order to harm or hinder the occupying forces.

We took any opportunity to drop a few sugar cubes in the fuel tanks of army vehicles or spread bent nails on the highways. These nails were made sharp at both ends and then bent in such a way that they would always have one of the points sticking up. They were then immersed in water so they would rust and lose their shine. We spread these contraptions on the roads after dark while cycling along the bicycle path at the side of the highway.

I spent the summer of 1940 after graduation at Hillegersberg; arriving in the early summer the boating season had already started. There were still very few boats in the water but everyone was busily scraping, sanding, varnishing and painting their boats; the atmosphere around the boats was surprisingly carefree. The Germans were nowhere in sight and were, if not forgotten, temporarily put out of our minds. My group of friends had decided we would go on an all-summer trip with four boats through the canals north from Hillegersberg to three or four popular lakes in the region, and then back via a different route. Five of us who traveled together in a cabin cruiser included Boy Sissingh, Josh, me and Boy's two sisters, Jannie and Beth. The cabin cruiser, though a little cramped, could sleep the three men, Boy, Josh and me, while Jannie and Beth preferred to sleep in a tent on the shore.

Gathering the necessary supplies was not easy and we had to rely largely on my friends' mothers who stocked us with rationed supplies such as tea, coffee, butter, etc. that could only be bought with coupons. We figured that we could get any other supplies from the farms on the way. After all, we were young and did not foresee any problems. We set out as soon as we had everything we thought we needed. When you travel through canals you have to go through many locks which often cause long delays. At most locks commercial barges had priority, and there was usually not enough room for anything else when a huge barge was occupying a lock. The waiting did not bother us much; it gave us the opportunity to go sightseeing and, if the time was right, to have a beer in one of the pubs. Sometimes we even let our turn go by if we wanted to spend more time ashore.

Eventually, after traveling about fifty or sixty kilometres we arrived at the 'Kaagmeer', a small lake close to the cities of Wassenaar and Leiden. At that time it was the place where most of the well to do had their large and expensive looking boats usually moored alongside a houseboat owned by the same person. They looked down their noses at our noisy group with very ordinary boats and dressed like pirates. We found the atmosphere rather stuffy and after a few days decided to move on to the next lake, the 'Loosdrecht', a much larger lake mainly used by young people such as us, all looking for fun. Here we stayed till the end of our holidays. By simply not discarding the old tea or tealeaves or the old coffee and coffee grounds, we were able to make our tea and coffee last until the end of our trip. We just added a little more fresh tea or coffee to the pot and poured on hot water. We sailed all day and in the evening went into town and enjoyed ourselves where all the action was. In retrospect it seems amazing to observe that we never saw a German soldier and I don't think that any of us even thought of the German occupation while on vacation. We never read or even saw a newspaper the entire summer and battery-operated radios had not yet been invented.

We had beautiful weather all summer but towards the end of August we were all ready to set out for home. Going along the canals in through farmer's fields was fun and very peaceful. One day we saw some ducks swimming in the canal ahead of us. I motioned to the others to be very quiet and stay out of sight as we approached. I watched them from a corner of the cabin and when we came alongside, I quickly stuck my arm out and managed to grab one of the ducks by the neck and haul it into the boat. The others did not seem to be disturbed and quietly went on their way behind us. The next two nights we had roast duck for dinner, quite a luxury and a welcome change from our menu over the past two months. I shudder as I relate this story since it is something that I would never do under normal circumstances. But during the war when we were perpetually hungry it seemed a reasonable thing to do and all my friends thought that it was a great idea.

As we came nearer to home, the mood among us became more serious and the conversations were increasingly about the war and how we could help the allies. We all had great ideas, none of them very practical and some of them impossible. Nevertheless, our minds were constantly occupied by the war and someone would invariably start talking about it. So, by the time we reached home, we had changed from the carefree people who had set out on the trip to five individuals completely occupied by the war and the German occupation. The effects of the war were being felt and the presence of the occupation forces had become increasingly noticeable. The feeling that there was nothing that we could do was frustrating to say the least. We dealt with our frustration by forming our own little resistance group, keeping it small and not letting anyone join until we knew that he or she was to be trusted and not inclined to talk to people outside the group. We decided that a new recruit would only get to know one of us and we pledged that we would never put anything on paper that could lead to arrest. We took these security measures because whole groups had been arrested in the past: within the group everybody knew everybody else and members had been arrested with a complete list of phone numbers in their pockets.

Most of the German soldiers in Holland at that time were older veterans not deemed suitable to send to the fighting front. Others were mainly security forces such as Gestapo, Sicherheits Dienst (SD), S.S., (S.S., short for 'Waffen SS', an elite German division often used to assist the Gestapo). The most hated of all the forces were the members of the Dutch National Socialist Party who paraded in uniforms similar, except for colour, to the German ones. As far as we were concerned they were traitors.

During the summer's boat trip Boy Sissingh, his two sisters, and I had become good friends. Boy suggested that I should move in with him, having already asked his mother for her permission. I liked the idea very much and gratefully accepted. I think my guardian was probably relieved that I was going to leave, since he knew that I was not getting along very well with his son.

Boy's father, Mr. Sissingh was captain of a large ocean-going vessel and when the war broke out he was at sea. Across the street lived another family whose father was also a captain of a vessel owned by the same company. He too was overseas when the war broke out. Neither family had heard from them since the onset of the war.

Chapter Four

Going to Sea, a Courier for the Secret Service

I had to complete a one-year apprenticeship on board a vessel before I could write my next exam. This now became my first priority and I regularly scoured the jobs offered in the local paper. I spotted an advertisement by a shipping company in a town located in the extreme northeast of Holland looking for a deckhand for one of their coasters. I phoned the company, was accepted right away, and was to report within three days to the captain of the "Meteor", a three hundred-ton coaster moored in the harbour of Delfzijl in the northeast corner of Holland next to the German border. The next couple of days were spent roaming the ship's chandlers to buy suitable clothes that were by then in short supply and only available with a permit. The third day I boarded a train in Rotterdam on my way to Delfzijl. It was, for Holland, a long journey with many transfers; I arrived in late afternoon and went directly to the harbour to look for 'The Meteor'. I had no trouble finding her and reported to the captain. He signed me up and so I became one of the five men crew consisting of the captain, first mate, the cook and one able-bodied seaman and me, a deckhand. The seaman and I each had a bunk in the foxhole (in the bow of the ship for those not familiar with the nautical term). Our shifts were to be twelve hours on and twelve off. My wage was to be twenty-five guilders per month with overtime. Captains knew that we had to complete a one-year apprenticeship and usually took advantage of it by paying us the absolute minimum, and sometimes even less than that, as in my case. But I didn't care and was happy to have a job. I was looking forward to being at sea at last as well as the prospect of going to a neutral country, Sweden, where we were to pick up a load of lumber.

The ship left the next morning and I discovered that the twelve-hour shifts only applied when we were at sea. Our route took us through the Kiel Canal, in North Germany, where we had to pass inspection by the German authorities. We had to go through two locks at which time it was 'all hands on deck', as was also the case during mooring and loading operations. I should also mention the hours we had to spend pumping water out of the foxhole, our 'bedroom' where the other deckhand and I had our bunks. The ship readily took on water during rough weather and we had plenty of that! The trip took about a month and when we came back to port, I was discharged and told that the ship would be ready to sail again in a week and to report back in six days.

When I got home and told my friends that I had been to Sweden and that I was probably going there again on my next trip, Mrs. Sissingh suggested that I take a letter to her husband for mailing in Sweden. I thought that this was a great idea and suggested that the people across the street also might want to write a letter to their father and husband. Little did I realize the significance at the time, because this was the beginning of my involvement with the war. Mailing the letters did not pose any problem and when I came back from my second trip, there were four more letters waiting for me to take to Sweden.

One day, when I was between voyages, Boy asked me to go for a stroll with him after dinner. I immediately sensed he had something important to discuss with me. He told me that he had come in touch with someone who was connected to an organization with contacts in England. When Boy had mentioned to him that I had taken letters to mail in Sweden he suggested that Boy ask me if I would be willing to take maps and drawings to Sweden. I could either just mail it or else phone a certain number and someone would meet me and take the documents off my hands. I was exuberant; finally a chance to be involved, if only on a small scale, so I accepted right away. "Does he know my name?" I asked. Boy replied, "No, he doesn't want to know your name and he also doesn't want me to know his name. In fact, when I was introduced to him, I had the feeling that he used a false name". This made the proposal even more to my liking, as it gave me the feeling that I was dealing with a professional.

The day before I left to go back to the boat, Boy handed me a large brown envelope that I stuck in my duffel bag between my clothes. When I had gone on board the first time, I had noticed a German sentry on the dock who randomly inspected the luggage that was brought onto the ship. He didn't stop my colleague or me; he inspected mainly the officers and didn't bother with us lesser folks. I therefore decided to change into my work clothes before I left the train station to go to the boat. It was the right decision because to my relief the sentry, as on previous occasions, was only spot checking the better dressed crew members.

We left for Sweden with an empty ship and again went for a load of lumber. I liked this because it meant that we would again spend at least three days loading, which gave the crew plenty of opportunities to go ashore and for me do what I had to do. I decided that I would phone the number given to me, for then at least I knew that it would arrive at its intended destination. The person I contacted spoke in English and said that he would be there in a couple of hours and to wait for him at a café closest to the railway station. He would have the collar of his coat turned up and a newspaper in his right hand. I was to give a big yawn as soon as I saw him come in.

Everything happened as planned, without a hitch; I sat in a booth facing the door and there were only a few other customers having a cup of coffee and reading newspapers. My contact walked straight up to me and asked me in Swedish if he could join me. Nobody paid the slightest attention to us. He ordered a coffee and I slipped the envelope to him under the table. He put the envelope beside him on the seat and covered it with his hat. The place was poorly lit and ideal for such an exchange. After a while we shook hands and I left, feeling happy to have completed my mission successfully.

When I came home from this second trip, I learned that there was an opening on the 'Noordwijk', a five thousand-ton freighter sailing out of Rotterdam. Captain Sissingh was on a ship belonging to the same company as the Noordwjik. I immediately applied for the opening and was accepted. Now I would not have to make those long train trips to Delfzijl; my pay was considerably better and I only had to work eight hours a day. My accommodation also greatly improved as I was now going to have a bunk in a cabin for two. It was now the middle of December, 1941 and we were scheduled to leave in the middle of January. It started to snow just before Christmas and by the time it stopped there were about ten centimetres of snow on the ground. This was my first real experience with snow; I thought it was great stuff and we had lots of fun throwing snowballs and "playing" in the snow.

Mrs. Sissingh had somehow obtained a turkey from a farm and Christmas dinner was the absolute luxury of roast turkey stuffed with chestnuts together with all the usual trimmings. We felt very fortunate and privileged because in 1941 food was becoming very scarce. We had already started to make our own rye bread by boiling the dough in a large juice can, and were making our own sauerkraut. Potatoes and vegetables were still available but one needed coupons for bread, butter, meat and eggs and we could only buy a very limited quantity of these items.

Once more I was asked to take a bundle of papers to Sweden. I say papers because I had no idea what these large envelopes contained, and I didn't want to know. I always figured that the less I knew the better. For about a week before the ship was due to sail I came on board almost every day to carry out maintenance work. We scrubbed the decks, painted the cabins, polished the brass in the wheelhouse, etc. There was a German sentry on board all day, and I soon learned that there would be a sentry on board during the entire trip, even in neutral Swedish waters. This was, of course, against international regulations, but who was going to stop them! At that time the Germans were still the winning side and Sweden thought it wise not to protest. They had agreed to cooperate with Germany in exchange for not being occupied like their neighbours, Norway and Denmark. I even saw German warships escorting a convoy of freighters loaded with iron ore sailing through Swedish waters destined for Germany. Sometimes freighters were escorted by Swedish warships as well. These freighters were equipped with anti-aircraft guns, as was ours, and also carried enough personnel, i.e. soldiers, to man these guns even though the ship was in neutral Swedish waters. The presence of the soldiers made my courier activities more difficult and I had to be very careful when taking the contraband on board. This time I was given three large bundles and took one bundle aboard at a time. I also timed coming on board to coincide with the time that the soldiers were having lunch and distracted. I found what proved to be a perfect hiding place underneath the floorboards of my closet. Nobody would ever find them with a cursory inspection of the cabins where we slept.

In the third week of January, 1942, we sailed out of Rotterdam late in the afternoon as part of a convoy of about eight freighters escorted by three German torpedo boats. Early the next morning we were attacked by approximately seven Hurricane airplanes. They came in flying very low above the water and, even before we could see them, bullets were flying and bombs had been released and were skipping on the water. The Germans had not fired a single round before the planes were up and gone. Miraculously only one of the ships was hit, in the bow, by one of the bombs. A few bullets went through our wheelhouse but there were no casualties. One had to admire the skill of the pilots as they had barely cleared the ship's masts; one daredevil even flew between the smokestack and the antenna strung between the masts. It made us feel very good to see our allies in action; despite the fact that we had been attacked, but I am sure that the Germans on board did not feel the same way.

We stopped at Hamburg where we loaded some freight and then on to Oxelösund, south of Stockholm, our final destination. A fierce wind was blowing from the northeast and the temperature was about minus 40 degrees C. The harbour was starting to freeze over and it took us a long time to get alongside because of the large chunks of ice between the ship and the dock, which had to be pushed out of the way by hand. There was an icebreaker constantly breaking up the ice in the harbour to enable the ships to move around. There were a total of eighteen ships in the harbour and by this time there was no way out through the narrow passage to the open ocean. After unloading we had to be assisted by the icebreaker and a couple of tugs to move us to somewhere in the centre of the harbour. This was where we stayed for the next few months during which time I had plenty of opportunities to dispatch my three parcels. The days were spent chipping and scraping the rust off the hull while standing on the ice. We stood inside six-ply paper bags, in which potatoes had been delivered from the supplier in town, to keep our feet from freezing. As it became a bit warmer we started to paint the hull and by the time we were able to leave the harbour the ship looked like new. It was the end of April before the ice in the harbour could be broken up so that we could leave. Two icebreakers led all eighteen ships at the same time to the open water. We got back to Rotterdam during the second week of May.

While I was away much had changed and the underground movement was starting to take shape. There had been a few casualties, which was only to be expected as we were all rank amateurs when it came to this kind of activity. Our little group had not been compromised and had actually become quite professional, carefully observing potential members before asking them to join. One of them was a chap named of Peter de Beer. He had white blond hair and soon we referred to him as 'White Pete'. Another new recruit was Boy Sissingh's youngest sister Jannie. She was to prove to be one of the best underground workers we ever had. The girls were mainly involved in courier duties: taking messages, either written or verbal, and other items from one person to another.

I made two more trips on the Noordwijk, each time taking bundles of papers to Sweden. On the way back on one of these trips, we were in convoy on the North Sea. It was bright daylight when we suddenly heard the sound of aircraft; I looked up and saw what looked like bombers directly overhead. We assumed that these were Allied aircraft flying back from Germany after dropping their bombs. Then we saw a large number of little dots below the planes and not long thereafter there were explosions all around us. The water seemed to be boiling but, miraculously not one single ship was hit. I came to the conclusion that these bombers had not dropped their load in Germany so were now on their way back to their base in England, when they spotted the convoy and decided to get rid of their bombs. Later, I decided that their chances of hitting one of the ships were very small. It was like trying to drop a pea from six feet trying to hit a nickel on the floor!

I had now served enough time as an apprentice to write my next exam. I concentrated on my studies and locked myself away for a few months. I really wanted to pass the exam so that I could get a job as a deck officer. I wrote the exam in October and passed, but it wasn't till next March, 1943 that I managed to get a job as third mate on the Beverwijk, owned by the same company as the Noordwijk. All the ships' names ended with 'wijk' and the company was known as the 'Wijkline'. We were to sail in a few weeks and I was able to use that time to clean and paint my cabin, and to observe the movements of the German sentry on board. He got to know my face and I always gave him a friendly greeting. Every day I brought a small suitcase on board containing a few clothes and some sandwiches. I would open the suitcase very demonstratively, making sure that he saw me. A few days before sailing I started to bring on the documents for my friend in Sweden, but after I got it all on board and well hidden, we got word that our destination was going to be Helsinki in Finland, not Sweden. This was quite a blow because it meant that I would not be able to deliver the documents. I discussed it with my friends and we decided that it was much safer to keep them on board.

I had never been to Finland before and enjoyed the new experience. It was still very cold, about minus thirty degrees Celsius. While in Helsinki, the second mate and I decided to try out a Finnish bath. There are plenty of bath houses in the Scandinavian countries and we were in for quite a surprise. We had a choice of about twenty different types of bathhouses and not knowing one type of bath from another we just picked one at random. We were each given a clean towel and directed to a room; when we entered we were greeted by a lady who told us to take all our clothes off, go to the sauna for about ten minutes and then proceed to the next room where she would be waiting for us. The idea of stripping and then appear before a woman whom we had never seen before was something new to us and made us feel very uneasy and set us wondering whether we should just forget about the whole thing. But curiosity got the better of us and we did as we were told. When we came to the next room she told us to stand inside one of the circles painted on the floor and to slowly turn around and keep turning until she told us to stop. As soon as we stood in our circle she turned the warm water on us, soon to be followed by very cold water, then warm again, and cold again, and so on for the about ten minutes. She was then joined by another lady who came in with two long fir boughs. She handed one of the boughs to the other lady. We were told to keep turning around and they proceeded to whip us with the boughs from the neck down and back up again for the about five minutes. They seemed to enjoy doing this to two strangers who had obviously never had such an experience before; I am not sure if I enjoyed it as much as they did. My whole body was covered with red marks and I felt as if I was on fire as we made our way back to the dressing room. Later, on our way back to the ship, we felt quite invigorated and could no longer feel the cold until after the effects of our 'bath' had worn off.

Our next voyage was to Sweden and I was able to hand the papers to my Swedish contact. We were attacked again on the North Sea and again did not suffer any casualties. During this trip we lost three of our crew members who went on shore in Sweden and never returned. Sweden was the only country in Western Europe that was not occupied by the Germans. As long as the Germans were winning side, Sweden cooperated with Germany as much as possible. Consequently refugees who sought asylum in

Sweden were routinely turned over to the German consulate in Sweden who would then ship them back to Germany, but by 1943 the tide had turned and Sweden was no longer turning the asylum seekers back to the Germans.

When we arrived back to port in Holland we heard that Dutch ships would no longer be going to Sweden because of the deserters. When I reported to the office, I was told that I was to transfer to the Randwijk in the position of Second Mate. The Randwijk was an older and smaller ship but, of course, I was pleased with the unexpected promotion. Our pipeline to Sweden was now severed and it meant the end of our document traffic. I pondered whether I should resign to do full time underground work. I was aware that there had been Allied agents operating in Holland and I decided to remain on the boat and perhaps, just may-be, get the opportunity to somehow go to Sweden and then to England. By this time the food situation in Holland had worsened considerably; meat, butter, sugar, even lard were in very short supply especially in the large cities. Every day one would see more and more people leaving the cities in the early morning for the surrounding farms to try to buy potatoes and vegetables. A farmer would sometimes even part with a piece of meat if you were lucky. Later on, even potatoes became scarce and people had to resort to eating tulip bulbs. Since I had been on board ships most of the time where we always seemed to have plenty to eat, I never experienced the food shortages myself, but every time I was ashore I heard plenty of stories. Everybody seemed to be pre-occupied with food and eating. Quantity rather than quality became the main concern.

Chapter Five

Jumping Ship and Swimming Ashore to Sweden: 1943

Our next voyage was to Finland again, but further north.

This destination meant that we had to go through the group of islands between Stockholm and the coast of Finland. I had been through these islands before and knew that there were frequent pilot changes on this stretch. During a pilot change the ship would go dead slow for a while which, I thought, would perhaps give me the opportunity to bail out.

We left Rotterdam on October 20, 1943. Again we were attacked by a number of low flying Hurricanes; it seemed that the Allies always knew that a convoy had left Rotterdam. On our way to Finland I became increasingly anxious about the prospect of jumping ship and my mind was constantly occupied in trying to visualize how I could do it. I grew more confident and was almost certain that it could be done. At last we arrived at the entrance of the island group and took our first pilot on board. It was about two o'clock in the afternoon and still broad daylight but I knew that it would be dark by the time the next pilot came on board and if not, then certainly by the time the third pilot came on board.

I calculated that the third exchange would take place after midnight and I hoped that the German sentries would have gone to bed by then. When we entered the Baltic Sea they were no longer on duty to man the anti-aircraft guns; for them it was almost like a holiday cruise until such time as we entered the German waters again. Our third mate would be on duty until midnight when I took over the graveyard shift. Everything seemed to be in my favour and I decided to wait till the third pilot exchange that should take place just before midnight when the third mate was still on duty. I would not raise any suspicion if I was on the aft deck where the pilot would come on board. I spent most of the evening in my cabin and went up to the bridge to check our position and asked the pilot when he thought the next exchange would be. 'About eleven thirty' he said which I figured would be the ideal time to go overboard. I went back to the cabin to check to see for the last time that I didn't have any incriminating articles left around that could cause the other officers trouble if they were found by the Germans. About a quarter past eleven I went to the aft deck and pretended to check that everything was in order. One of the German soldiers was leaning on the railing smoking a cigarette and watching one of the hands lowering the rope ladder in preparation for the exchange of pilots. I was about twenty feet behind him and when I heard the ship's engine come to a stop, I threw a rope over the railing, lowered it to the water and fastened it with a couple of loops around a guy line which was fastened onto the railing. Nobody seemed to pay the slightest attention to me. Soon I could see the pilot boat approaching and in the distance a small light that I surmised came from the pilothouse onshore. The new pilot came on board and the old one went down the rope ladder and into the boat that sped away in the direction of the light. I heard the ring on the bridge to signal the engine room to resume full speed ahead. "It's now or never!" I thought, I went over the railing, lowered myself into the water, kicked off and swam a few strokes away from the boat to be as far as possible from the propeller. I still wore my cap and kept absolutely still until the ship was far enough away before starting to swim towards the light from the pilothouse. The water was very cold and it felt like I was being stung all over my body by a billion needles; the pilot house which looked only a few hundred yards away from the deck now looked so far away. I knew that I had to keep swimming hard to keep my arms and legs from going numb; I still had all my clothes and my shoes on and this made swimming very difficult. I am sure that the adrenaline was partly responsible for keeping my body warm and keeping me going. I kept telling myself to keep swimming, and once in a while I looked to see if I was still swimming in the right direction and getting any closer. I don't know how long I had been in the water but it was an intense relief when suddenly I felt bottom and walked the rest of the way ashore and to the pilothouse. 'I did it!' I thought and a feeling of intense satisfaction washed over me.

I knocked on the door and stepped in to face a couple of very surprised Swedish pilots who immediately realized what had happened and how I came to be knocking at their door. In fact, one of the pilots was the one I had spoken to on the bridge earlier that evening. I took my clothes off right away and then was taken downstairs to a huge wood-burning stove. The heat felt wonderful and I was soon dry and warm. The pilots gave me some underwear, a shirt, and a pair of pants and then put a huge bowl of beef stew in front of me. I hadn't eaten beef for a long time as it was very scarce at that stage of the war. They told me that I was not the first one to step into the pilot house dripping with water, and that they had to report my arrival to the police in Stockholm who would then come to pick me up. That was fine with me because I was now in neutral territory. They gave me a pack of cigarettes and told me use one of the spare cots and have a sleep because it would be much later before anybody came to pick me up. Before long I was asleep and when I woke my own dry clothes hung over a chair by my bed. The pilots had hung my wet clothes on a rack by the stove where they had dried during the night. I got dressed and went into the main room where they had breakfast ready for me. They treated me like a king; I couldn't have asked for better. After the years of German occupation when one had to be on guard all the time; listen to the news of the BBC while making sure that it couldn't be heard outside; to cope with a black-out in force so that no lights were visible from the house outside, and to live with the food rationing, etc. this was sheer luxury.

Later that morning a motor launch with two Stockholm police officers aboard pulled into the dock to take me to Stockholm. They explained to me that I would go to jail overnight and attend a hearing tomorrow when I would have to explain why I was in Sweden. They advised me to simply say: 'I am a political fugitive and I seek asylum.' I would then be free to go and would be directed to the Dutch authorities in Stockholm. When I arrived at the jail, I was directed to a general holding area and there much to my surprise was one of the crew from my ship with whom I had had a long conversation when he was at the wheel the previous day. He had jumped ship just after I did at the next pilot exchange and had been lucky enough to be picked up by the pilot boat a short time after he went into the water. He was a very educated crewmember who had obviously applied for the job for the specific purpose of leaving Holland to try and reach Sweden. His name was Ludo de Stoppelaar and we soon became the best of friends. Another 'inmate' who had heard us conversing in Dutch approached us and introduced himself as Wim Dinger. He told us that he had been working on a German ship and that he had gone ashore and asked for asylum when his ship was in Stockholm harbour.

Events went exactly the way we had been told by the police. After the formality in court, we were on our way to the Netherlands Foreign Office where we were registered and were then sent to the consulate where we were given money, clothes, toiletries, etc. They also gave us a temporary address where we could stay and were told that we would soon be shipped to a logging camp in the woods. The prospect of becoming a logger did not appeal to me at all. The next day I went to the British consulate and told them that I had been acting as a courier with documents that were handed over to a gentleman whom I contacted by phone; I gave them the telephone number. I also told them that I had jumped ship because of the fact that I would no longer be going to Swedish ports. They immediately knew what I was talking about and asked me to come back the next day when they would have a better idea what next to do with me. The following day I was subjected to a long interview and was told that they would contact me in a few weeks. The Dutch authorities would be contacted and told that I was to stay in Stockholm to await their decision.

The pocket money we received from the Dutch consulate wasn't very much and I decided to look for a temporary job. I told Ludo and Wim that I had contacted the British authorities because of my previous courier work with them and that I would not be going to the woods. They immediately decided to start looking for a job too, so that they no longer had to be at the mercy of the Dutch authorities. The three of us started our job hunting and by the end of the day we had all found ourselves a job. Ludo became a dishwasher in a restaurant and could not get over all the good-looking waitresses that he had seen there. I found a job as a bicycle boy delivering parcels all over the city. Wim had found himself a deluxe job; he had gone to the Netherlands Embassy where they happened to be looking for a butler. He even was provided with a separate suite just off the kitchen as accommodation in the embassy. We couldn't believe our luck!

The next day I went to the dispatch office and got my first assignment. The work was pretty steady and I was never in the office for very long before the next job came. Once in a while I had to take a bicycle pulling a cart behind loaded with boxes; Stockholm is a very hilly city and negotiating the hills dragging a heavy load behind me was not easy. I remember that one day, when I had one of these loads behind me I turned a corner onto a steep downhill. That is when I discovered that I had no brakes and the hill came out onto a very busy street. I was already going too fast to jump off my bike. All I could do was to start screaming at the top of my voice: "I have no brakes! I have no brakes!" Miraculously I sailed unscathed through both lines of traffic and started going uphill on the other end of the intersection. When I came to a stop I was shaking and perspiring and my heart was pounding.

Ludo came home carrying a large box that evening. He opened the box and proceeded to 'set the table' with paper plates and silverware that he had brought home from the restaurant where he worked. He then produced a large bowl with food and motioned me to sit down and start eating. He had brought everything, meat, potatoes, vegetables and even a desert. Did that ever hit the spot! Ludo suggested that I should drop in for lunch at his place every day; not only would I see his good looking co-workers but he would make certain that they would give me extra large portions. From then on, I would make certain that I was in the neighbourhood of the restaurant where he worked around lunchtime and I did get the huge portions he promised! I had to agree that his co-workers were indeed very pretty; and they seemed always to be extra nice to me.

In the evening we would quite often drop in on our friend, Wim Dinger at the embassy. The ambassador and his wife would be either having a dinner party at home or attending a dinner party elsewhere. One evening we dropped in on Wim while there was a dinner party in progress. Wim had to serve the drinks and while we were in his room he passed on to us many a tray of glasses with various kinds of cocktails. After dinner the ambassador's party decided to go elsewhere and we were left by ourselves in an empty house. By then we had had quite a bit to drink and we decided to go to a dance, but we realized that we would never be admitted dressed the way we were. Emboldened by the liqueur we had consumed, we decided to have a look in the ambassador's clothes closet. There were at least thirty suits hanging in the closet, enough to start a men's-wear store. We each picked a shirt, a tie and a suit and proceeded to get dressed for the dance. I was lucky, the clothes fitted me to a tee, but Wim, who was quite a bit heavier, barely managed to button up his pants and could not possibly button up his jacket. When I looked over to Ludo, I had to burst out laughing. Ludo was quite a bit smaller than me and his pants hung down in wrinkles on his shoes while his jacket must have been three sizes too large. He reminded me of Charlie Chaplin. When he saw himself in the mirror we all started to laugh and to wonder if we should forego the dance. But off we went and when we got there, there was a long line-up of people to buy tickets. Security guards were going up and down the line checking for people who had had too much to drink; anyone they found was sent home. As a consequence, everyone tried to be very quiet and only spoke in a hushed voice.

We had guessed that they were very strict and would not allow anybody who had had too much to drink into the dance hall, so we were all sucking on very strong peppermints to make sure that they could not smell anything on our breath. But when Ludo for some reason suddenly burst out laughing, one of the guards pulled him out and told him to open his mouth. And here was Ludo standing on his toes in front of the big six foot guard blowing in his face, all the while saying: "peppermint, peppermint!" We had trouble containing our laughter but we all managed to slip through and enter the dance hall.

I found a girl that I particularly liked and after I had danced with her four or five times, she asked me if I would like to walk her home and come in for a coffee. I couldn't believe my ears; how lucky could I get and I eagerly accepted her invitation. Just before we were to enter her house, she said that I had to be very quiet because to reach her room we had to go through her parents' bedroom! Right away I was not so eager to go inside anymore, but she encouraged me and said that it was quite all right. As we walked through her parents' bedroom, her dad woke up and said: "Is that you Brigitte?" "Yes dad," she answered "and I have someone with me." "Please be very quiet," he said, and that was it. I couldn't believe my ears. I had visions of an angry father chasing me out of the house with an iron poker or something similar. But nothing happened; we had a coffee and a chat and after about an hour or so, she said, "let's go to bed" and told me where I could sleep. She even gave me a pair of pyjamas I could wear, probably her dad's. After I was in bed, she came in and lay down beside me, kissed me goodnight, turned around and went to sleep. And soon I was asleep too. In the morning her dad came in with a couple of cups of coffee and asked us if we had a good time at the dance.

I suddenly realized that I was still wearing the ambassador's clothes, so I excused myself and said that I had to report for work soon, got dressed, thanked Brigitte for the nice evening and left. I never saw her again and have often wondered if my experience was something quite normal for Sweden. Back at the embassy, I quickly put my own clothes back on and asked Wim to put the ambassador's clothes back in the closet. "Don't worry," he said, "he'll never miss them and I'll put everything back when they leave the house next time." Ludo had gone home with Wim and was still sound asleep on the floor, still in his suit and tie. He had only taken his shoes off. It had been quite a night!

A few weeks later, I received a call from the Dutch consulate; they wanted to see me as soon as possible. I went there right away and was told to contact George and was given his telephone number to call. When I called him, he asked me to meet him at a certain address and I went there right away; the address was next to the British consulate. George told me then that there were plans in the making to fly me to England, soon; but that this could mean anywhere between a week and two months, or possibly longer. He then asked me if I would be interested in working for Intelligence and explained what he had in mind. I was elated and accepted right away. This is exactly what I had been dreaming about and I could scarcely believe that it was now going to happen. I was to start the next day if I wanted to; "Yes, I can start to-morrow, where do I go". He told me to come back the next morning and he would take me to where I would be working.

I hurried back to the dispatch office and told my employer that I would no longer be working there as of now. I received my pay and left. When I had first arrived I had been given a clothing allowance but since I could just wear my old clothes for my bicycle job, I had not bought any. I would certainly need them now so I spent the rest of the day buying some decent clothes and enjoyed a good dinner at the restaurant where Ludo worked. I told him my great news. He told my waitress to give me an extra large portion and came out the kitchen himself a couple of times to talk to me. He suggested we went to Wim's place that night to celebrate. After dinner I went home, changed into my new clothes, and went to the Dutch embassy where Wim worked and told him my news. A short time later

Ludo arrived; there was a dinner at the embassy and Wim had to leave us to serve the drinks. Once in a while he would stick his head around the door to give us a tray of drinks and a tray of snacks. After the dinner party including the hosts had left for the theatre, Ludo suggested that we should go out again wearing the ambassador's clothes. Wim thought that it was a great idea but when I said that I would not join them they both changed their mind and decided to stay put and go to bed early. I was not about to have a hangover on the first day of my new job!

When I reported for work the next day, George took me to the room where I was going to work. However from then on I had to use a different entrance so George took me back outside and showed me where I should come in. We sat down in my new 'office' and he explained my job to me. Apparently, the German counter espionage had been trying to infiltrate by having their agents jump ship, as I had done, and pose as political refugees. My job was to screen those that had jumped ship and had voiced their desire to go to England to work as a spy for the Allies. There was a ten-page questionnaire to use as a guide, we had a short discussion about it, and he gave me a sum of money to take my 'clients' for lunch, dinner or other entertainment and left. I never saw him again.

I studied the questionnaire and then someone came in with my first candidate. At first I asked most of the questions on the papers handed to me but soon I started using my own questions. I found that the agents sent out by German intelligence were easy to spot. The Dutch agents especially would soon give themselves away and after a bit of probing I was pretty certain when a man was on the wrong side. Of course,

I did not let on that I was suspicious but played along to give the impression that he would be someone of value to the Allies. The German agents were not much better. It took me a little longer to unravel them because I was not so familiar with the situation in Germany. After a while I developed a sort of a sixth sense that served me well. When I was pretty sure that I had a suspicious person, I would tell him that the Allies would certainly be interested in his services, and then I turned him over to British intelligence. During that time, of the three suspects I turned over to British Intelligence, one never left Sweden and the other two were flown to England. Later I heard that one of them was hanged and the other was confined in a compound for the duration of the war.

Christmas came and went and towards the end of January I was told that within a few days I would be flown to England from Gothenburg. I was to be at the Stockholm train station by 10 a.m. the next day where somebody would meet me. I joined up with three others at the station; we boarded the train and were on our way. The others were not very talkative which suited me fine as I didn't want them to start asking me questions; neither did I want to know anything about them. We were each given a room in a hotel in Gothenberg and were told to wait for instructions to be given to us every day between five and six in the evening. The rest of the time we were free to do as we wished.

The second day I received a call and was told to be in the lobby in ten minutes where I would be picked up. The same group of people who were in the train were in the lobby as well; we were driven to the airport where we were each given a flight suit, boots, a helmet and an oxygen mask and instructed to go into the waiting room. At about 9 p.m. we were told to don our flying gear and await further instructions. An hour later it was a terrible letdown when we were told that the flight had been cancelled and were driven to the hotel again. On the drive back we learned that, since most of the Allied bombers were in southern Germany, there were too many German fighters available to patrol the skies above the North Sea, which would have made the flight across very dangerous. This routine was repeated for the next two days and I was beginning to wonder if we were ever going to England, but on the fourth night we were told that the flight was on. We donned our flight gear and walked across the tarmac to the waiting aircraft. It was a Liberator stripped of all its weaponry and ammunition.

There were six passengers including the four of us; we climbed on board, sat down and buckled ourselves up, and there was barely enough room. I should explain that the flight suits consisted of pants, jackets, boots and helmet, all made from leather and sheepskin-lined which made us quite 'voluminous'! We quickly took off and we were on our way; as we looked down we could see the lights of Gothenburg below us for quite a while as we steadily gained altitude. Breathing started to become difficult and we were told to put on our oxygen masks and to hook up to the oxygen. When we were above twenty thousand feet, the aircraft set course to the west. The trip was quite uneventful and, a few hours later the pressure on our ears increased as we descended to land in England.

I will never forget the wonderful feeling that came over me, almost four years after the Germans occupied my country, finally to have arrived on the other side of the water and on the side of our Allies! The landing strip lights appeared and shortly after we were on the ground. As soon as the engines were turned off, the door opened and a lady in air force uniform came aboard and welcomed us with: "Good morning gentleman, welcome in Scotland. Please follow me"! It sounded like music to my ears and almost too good to be true. The flight gear which kept us so warm on our flight over, now started to become too warm and as soon as we were inside we took it all off and returned it. There was hot coffee, tea, chocolate, and sandwiches; also trays with packages of cigarettes and we were told to take as many as we wanted. Sheer heaven!

Chapter Six

England and Training for the Special Forces: 1944

After a shower and a hearty breakfast we were driven to Glasgow where we boarded the train to London. I was full of anticipation of things to come. What a letdown when I was taken to the 'Patriotic School' in London for security clearance. It appeared I might be there for as long as a month or more. The Royal Victoria Patriotic Building was originally built as an orphanage for dependents of service men lost in the Crimean War. The building was requisitioned during the First World War and became London's third General Hospital. The hospital was closed in 1938. During the Second World War the building became home to MI 5(Military Intelligence) and MI 6 and was used as a detention and interrogation centre with prison cells and various 'truth extracting' apparatus. Rudolph Hess was among the reluctant guests to enjoy its hospitality. All the windows of the building were barred and the front door, the one and only door out of the building, was guarded twenty-four hours a day.

Thank goodness the meals were good and we could get as many cigarettes as we wanted! Once or twice a day each of us would be called on the intercom to report to one of the interrogating rooms, there to be interrogated once again by one of the security officers. The rest of the time we played a lot of bridge with people of all nationalities. Once I sat at the same table with a partner, who, as I later found out was one of the eight best bridge players in France. He was annoyed at my way of bidding and every time I failed to bid according to the rules he would give me a long-winded lecture and reprimand. Before long I excused myself and left; he seemed to look relieved!

On the fourteenth day there my name was called as usual on the intercom to report again to one of the interrogation rooms. However, this time, after a few questions, I was told that I was security cleared and that I now was free to go. The Dutch authorities had been told of my pending release and arrived to pick me up. I was driven to the Netherlands House where I was officially welcomed into England. I was issued a battle dress, army boots, and a beret, booked into a hotel and told that I would be contacted quite soon. I was also told that I would get an invitation from Queen Wilhelmina! Wow! The next few days I spent sightseeing; I walked around London for many hours, especially in the parks, and in particular Hyde Park. I was still overwhelmed by this new situation I was in and the total freedom to go where I pleased, which strangely enough was something that I had to get used to again.

A few days later I received my invitation to tea from the adjutant of the queen and told I would be picked up at a certain hour on the day specified. I was told that the queen was going to ask me to join her staff and that I was not to use the word 'NO' in my answer, but instead to say something like: "I am very honoured your majesty.....etc". I was driven to her residence in the countryside about twenty miles outside London; the house was very modest in pleasant surroundings. I was welcomed by a lady, and my thoughts were spinning: was this the queen herself? Should I address her with 'your majesty? What if it isn't the queen? As these questions were racing through my mind. I decided that the safest way would be to address her with 'Madame'. This may sound strange to the reader but if one has never been head to head with the queen of your country, a person you have only seen on official photographs or on stamps, and then usually adorned with a crown, I am sure that you will begin to appreciate my predicament.

Our group were led through the garden to a patio next to the house where a quite informal gathering had formed in a circle with the queen. This time I was sure! I discovered later that most of the people in the group were also recent arrivals from Holland. I went up to the queen, bowed and she shook my hand and welcomed me. During the tea she asked each of us questions, mostly to do with the situation in Holland. It became obvious that she was intensely interested in the wellbeing of her people and already knew a lot about the situation in Holland. After she asked me a few questions she said that she wanted to speak to me alone afterwards. I thought, this is when she is going to ask me the question! I was correct; she did ask me to join her staff. I replied that I was very honoured, and then I explained to her that it was my desire to go back to Holland and work with the underground movement. She immediately agreed that this was far more important than remaining in England and then questioned me extensively about the underground movement. We talked together alone for almost half an hour and at the end she shook my hand and wished me Godspeed. It had been a very pleasant and emotional afternoon.

A few days later, much to my surprise, I received a phone call to tell me that I was to be the third officer on a ship that was now in Liverpool being unloaded. I was totally puzzled and very disappointed too! Had they not taken note of my wishes during the interview at the Netherlands House? Were they not aware that I wanted to go back to Holland? Perhaps I should have accepted the queen's offer. There was no alternative but to go to Liverpool. When I picked up my train ticket, I reiterated my wish to go back to Holland, rather than working in the merchant navy. I was told my wishes had been passed on to the proper channels, but there had been no reply, therefore it had been decided to send me back to the merchant navy, for which I was trained, rather than to wait any longer.

So, I traveled to Liverpool, reported to the captain of the ship and was shown my cabin. Reluctantly I started to tidy up and unpack my clothes and change into my merchant navy uniform. Two days later, an army officer came aboard who wanted to talk to me. He introduced himself as Kas de Graaf and told me that he was a representative of an organization that sent agents to Holland, by boat, submarine or parachute and wanted to know if I would be interested. "YES! Of course I am interested!" So, with much more enthusiasm, I changed back into my army uniform, packed my belongings, said good-bye to the ship's captain and was on my way! De Graaf himself had only recently arrived in England by way of Belgium, France, and Spain. He had been very involved with covert activities and knew the situation in Holland very well. In London, Kas took me to his office where I was introduced to his boss, General van Oorschot and two other staff. The general welcomed me into his organization and explained that I would start my training very soon. I was required to choose a name which I would be known by for the duration of my stay in England. I decided on 'Ben Saunders'.

I was asked to hand over my identification papers and in return, I was given one piece of paper that said something to the effect that if I was arrested for any reason, I should not be questioned but to immediately phone a certain number. The document was signed by a Major Dobson, second in command of 'Special Forces Netherlands', a section of S.O.E[1], which was directly under the command of SHAEF[2] and General Dwight D. Eisenhower. Directly under the command of S.O.E. were all the Special Forces including those from Norway, Denmark, Belgium, and France. The organization was the brainchild of Winston Churchill who wanted to 'set Europe ablaze' by arming the resistance forces behind the lines. The idea was to call these forces into action at a strategic moment. They were to cause maximum disruption behind the enemy lines by blowing up bridges, rail lines, tanks, etc. and to organize sabotage in every shape or form. Churchill kept a close tab on the operations and wanted to be informed of the state of affairs on a daily basis.

My first training course was at Ringway, close to Manchester where I was to learn parachute jumping. I was billeted separate from thousands of others who were also at Ringway to learn parachute jumping, in a small group of agents of many different nationalities who were being instructed separately from the regular paratroopers. The first day we were led through the 'parachute folding building', a huge place where hundreds of parachutes were folded at the same time led by commands by loudspeakers under the watchful eyes of inspectors on overhead walkways throughout

---

[1] S.O.E. – Special Operations Executive

[2] SHAEF- Supreme Headquarters Allied Expeditionary Forces

the building. It was truly an impressive sight! We were shown a piece of string used to tie the rigging line to the top of a parachute which had to be strong enough to pull the chute out of its bag, but at the same time supposed to break after the chute had fully extended so that no one would be left dangling underneath the aircraft. They assured us, to raise our confidence that there had never been a failure of a parachute not opening. Two days of ground training followed, jumping off a tower on a cable attached to your back. You landed on the ground and were barely back on your feet, when another cable on an electric winch was attached to your belt and pulled you along the ground to simulate a landing in a strong wind. As soon as you hit the release button the cable would detach itself. In reality, this is how you would have to detach yourself from the parachute that was being propelled along the ground by a strong wind. We were taught never to try to land on our feet but to keep our elbows in, hands on the ropes of the chute and with the knees bent to roll over onto our side and up on our feet again.

The third day was to be our first real parachute jump. When we got up in the morning, the entire area was fogged in and we were told that we would not be dropped by plane but out of a balloon. In the bus to the dropping field we all sang: 'Roll me over, roll me over, roll me over in the clover and do it again'. It was pure bravado because all of us looked rather pale! There were six of us and we were told to climb inside a big wooden box that had a hole in the centre with a thirty inch diameter and was about eighteen inches deep. We had been trained how to jump through a hole during the first two days of training. A 'rigging line' was connected to the top of the parachute strapped onto our back. Sitting sideways to the hole, we had to swing our legs into it, straighten out and at the same time push ourselves off. You had to do it just right or otherwise you would end up with a very sore nose! If you pushed too hard you would hit your face on the opposite side. If you didn't push off hard enough, your parachute would catch on the edge of the hole, tip you forward and you would hit your face on the opposite side.

The wooden box we were in was hanging underneath a big balloon that was attached by a steel cable to a winch on the ground. As soon as we were all aboard, the balloon started to ascend. It was eerily still around us and I was wondering how far up we were going. The dispatcher was busy attaching our rigging lines to the box; then the balloon stopped and 'action stations' was called. When it was my turn to jump, I moved to the edge of the box and at the command GO! I swung my legs into the hole, straightened out, pushed off and down and down I went...was that chute never going to open? I looked up and saw that my parachute was still stretched behind me and hadn't started to billow out; I started to wonder if it was ever going to open. Finally, after what seemed like a lifetime, it started to open, I could feel my speed decreasing, and then I was hanging in the air and no longer descending at free fall speed! It was a very pleasant and peaceful sensation and I wished that it would last forever. However, I was soon low enough to be able to see the ground through the fog. So, according to our instructions, it was elbows to the chest, knees bent, contact with the ground, roll on my side and up again, and it was all over! Our dispatcher told us that the balloons go up to eight hundred feet because it takes about one hundred and eighty feet before you gather enough speed for the chute to open. Believe me - it takes a long time to fall hundred and eighty feet! Normally, in a drop from a plane, the chute blows open almost immediately because of the slipstream of the aircraft.

On the way back on the bus we sang: "In the clover…" again, but this time it sounded much more sincere than before. The next three days we made four more jumps, all out of an airplane, three during the day and the last one at night. At night, due to the warm air rising from the ground, I came down very softly. The chutes that were used during the war were much smaller than those used by hobby parachute jumpers. The reason for this was to minimize the time in the air over enemy territory. A slow moving target would be all too easy to hit.

Back at the Cumberland Hotel I registered by my alias as 'Ben Saunders'. I was getting quite used to my assumed name. It was quite a strange sensation to suddenly become somebody else, a person without a history and not known by anybody. The next day I was visited by a lady officer who introduced herself as Captain 'so and so', though I now realized that almost everybody was using a false name. She taught me the basics of certain methods of coding and the need to develop a past for 'Ben Saunders'. She impressed on me that if you assume a false name that you need to have an assumed history attached to that name. It made a lot of sense! The following day she questioned me extensively about 'my past' and there were a lot of blank spots. It is not easy to become a person who only exists by name! It convinced me that Ben Saunders had to have a past and the importance of having an ironclad story in the event of an arrest.

Late that afternoon, I learned that I was to travel to Scotland the next day; Kas de Graaf would meet me at the train station. The next morning I took a cab to the station; Kas was already there and gave me the train tickets. 'I'll see you in a few weeks' were his last words and he left. I enjoyed my train trip and the prospect of my further training in Scotland; the countryside was a delight, especially the last part of the trip past Fort William through the highlands.

The next day I arrived in Mallaig, a small coastal village on the south shore of a 'loch', at the end of the rail line. In fact there had been four other chaps on the train going to the same place as me. All five of us boarded a motor launch that took us across the water. A lorry was waiting to take us to our training camp, about an hour away from where we landed. The countryside was absolutely bare, undulating terrain covered with what looked like moss. We saw no- one, only flocks of black sheep with white feet. In fact, during the three weeks that we were in camp we only once saw one herder in the distance.

The camp had been a hunting lodge before the war. Occasionally we saw large herds of deer, but only if we came over the brow of a hill before they had detected us. The next three weeks we were busy from six o'clock in the morning often till past midnight. There was basic commando training and also we were trained in 'silent killing', handguns and how to use them in close combat, the use of close range anti-tank weapons, etc. These exercises lasted the whole day until five o'clock with a short break for lunch; dinner break was from five till seven. During dinner the staff sergeant would come in and give us a broad overview of our night exercise. After dinner we were given the plan in detail so that we could draw up a detailed plan of execution. These night exercises would, for example, entail a raid on a German compound, surrounded by a fence with German sentries at each corner. We were to try to get to the sentries, eliminate them by 'silent killing' and gain entry to the compound to do as much damage inside the building as possible. The inside of the compound would be rigged with puppets coming down from the ceiling, a sound device would imitate loud German voices, gunshots, and then suddenly the lights would go out. The German sentries were staff, dressed in German uniform complete with helmets, and carrying a rifle with a bayonet. It was sometimes difficult, in the heat of the moment, to remember not to strike too hard and hurt them. Actually, while training us and demonstrating the different methods of silent killing, sometimes the trainer would go a little too far and put the student temporarily out of commission.

We were also trained to work with plastic explosives and how to disable different types of machinery, railroads, steel cables, tank tracks, and how to install different types of booby trap devices, even how to pick locks. We learned how to use stenguns, brenguns, bazookas, piat guns, and many other weapons. One day we all traveled by train to Arisaig, about ten miles south of Mallaig. It was here, that very significantly for me, we were taught how to get a steam locomotive in motion. At that time, I couldn't figure out for the life of me why we were being taught this, in the end it proved to be a very useful skill! There was a large house in Arisaig where the largest collection of handguns in the world was housed, or so we were told.

We spent a couple of hours disassembling and reassembling different types of guns that we picked off the shelves at random. After completing this task for twenty or thirty different types you could pretty well do them all without a problem. Pistol training different to the usual target practice: we were taught not to take aim but to shoot with the gun at chest height, pointing at the target, and always to fire twice in rapid succession. This technique was more effective since the targets always appeared suddenly and were always moving.

The days were long and very physically demanding; we were up sometimes till two or three in the morning. The terrain around us was peaty and mossy and always saturated with water. Apparently it usually rains three hundred and fifty days a year in that part of Scotland and it definitely did rain most of the time we were there. Consequently, we were issued with three battle dresses and three sets of underwear and since almost all of our exercises involved crawling or kneeling on the ground, we needed to change into dry clothes twice a day. The staff took care of our wet clothes drying them in a large coal fired dryer in a matter of a few hours. After three weeks at this camp, we all felt that we could handle any situation in the field and come out on top. The training at the parachute camp and in Scotland had made us physically very fit indeed and given us extreme confidence. When we boarded the train in Mallaig to return to London we, the five of us, acted as if we were complete strangers and once we parted I never saw any of the others again.

The next two weeks I stayed once more at the Cumberland Hotel, but this time I had a roommate who was to be on the same team as me. It was a very easy time compared to my experiences in Scotland; most of the time I stayed in my room to work on my cover story. Each time I reread it, I found gaps that could have got me into trouble. Occasionally a lady officer would come in to teach us the code we would be using in the field. We had to practise every day until we could code and decode very fast. The method for coding was simple and at the same time unbreakable. It was unbreakable because it was not based on a recurring sentence or poem, as almost all codes previously devised were, but on random groups of five letters.[3]

However, it was very unfortunate and a tragedy, that for a period of approximately one year, in 1943 and the beginning of 1944, all the agents dropped in Holland came into German hands and the British were ignorant of this fact. Obviously these changed security codes were more or less ignored.

At that time it was customary for all agents, or group of agents, to be dropped into the hands of a so called 'reception committee'. The result was that once the first agent was caught all subsequent ones were 'received' by the German intelligence and immediately whisked away. This scheme of deception became known as the 'England Spiel' and must have been one of the biggest blunders in the history of the British Intelligence. The jury is still out as to whose fault it was and it is doubtful whether a conclusion will ever be reached on this matter. It is believed that a few critical documents that might have shed some light on this blunder were destroyed. After all, there was a

---

[3] See addendum for full explanation of code.

suspicious fire right after the war at headquarters in Baker Street.

During those few weeks that I was in London I had a strange experience. One morning, I got up much earlier than usual, had a shower and got dressed. My roommate woke at that point and asked me where I was going. I said: 'I am going to have breakfast with the chap I met last night!'

'What chap last night?'

'The fellow I was talking to at Marble Arch'.

'You never talked to anyone but me last night'.

He then turned over and went back to sleep.

The person I was referring to having met at the Marble Arch was my buddy at the plantation when I was about ten years old. I had not seen him in all these years and we had decided to have breakfast together and chat about old times. I went to the restaurant and, sure enough he was there, and over our breakfast we talked up a storm. He was in navy uniform and told me an interesting story about how he came to be in the navy. Fleeing from the Japanese, he had been picked up by an Australian frigate, and eventually had landed in Britain where he joined the Dutch Navy. It was an amazing coincidence to meet a boyhood friend under such circumstances; even more extraordinary is that we had not 'seen' each other the night before! Both of us realized this at almost the same moment. Strange things happen! After breakfast we parted and I never saw him again.

Back in my hotel room my roommate asked me whom I had had breakfast with, and I told him my story still hardly believing it myself. After a long silence, and shaking his head in disbelief, he said, 'I was absolutely certain that you never spoke to anybody last night.'

Following this brief stay in London, I went to a large country estate, close to Islip, a small village about five kilometres north of Oxford. We were housed in a huge three-storied castle. I remember going over my cover story for the umpteenth time, but I don't remember receiving any training there. I also remember shooting rabbits and delivering them to the cook for rabbit stew. After a few days he told me that he did not want to see any more rabbits. So, instead of shooting them, I now practised creeping up on them to see how close I could get. I found out that if I stayed very close to the ground, a rabbit did not recognize me as a person and that I could come close enough to touch it while looking straight into its eyes. One day they seemed to be particularly shy and started moving away when I was still six or ten feet away. I was puzzled but suddenly heard noises straight behind and above me. When I looked around, I saw that a cow was right behind me! She must have been curious about that moving 'thing' in the grass. Needless to say, I got out of there in a hurry!

Every afternoon we had tea on the lawn with the major who was in charge of the place. His favourite trick was to bet every newcomer that he could hit a golf ball over the castle and pick it up on the other side. Since we were no more than fifty feet away from the three-storied castle everybody accepted the bet. He would proceed by putting the clearly marked ball on the lawn and hitting it almost straight up and over the castle, while those who had never seen this performance before looked on with utter disbelief! After those who had taken the bet had retrieved the ball on the other side, he would collect his money. One day the major asked me if I wanted to go with him to the dog races in Oxford. I declined and said that I didn't really care to watch such races. 'Neither do I' he replied, 'I'll just place my bets and then, when the races are on we will be in the pub, drinking beer'. This sounded very appealing to me so I accepted his invitation. On the way to Oxford he said, 'Why don't you give me a couple of pounds or whatever and I'll place the bets for you.' 'When the races are over, I'll go down and collect the money'. I looked in my wallet and found three pounds that I gave to him. We had a pleasant afternoon in the pub, swapping stories. When the races were over, he left, came back a few minutes later and handed me eight pounds and some change, my winnings for the afternoon. He had bet a lot more than three pounds; he never told me how much, but he had a big smile on his face. Sad to relate if he had a secret method for successful betting it was never revealed to me!

We were not very active during those few weeks, however I had the feeling that we were constantly being observed to look for telltale signs of any of us getting second thoughts about the mission we would shortly undertake. Perhaps showing signs of being distracted, becoming unresponsive during the day, or having restless nights would give an indication of our state of mind. We returned to London and told to go over our cover story once again. A few days later we were interrogated in detail about our fabricated past, exposing tiny gaps here and there. We didn't have to write them down but it made us realize that our story had to be complete in every detail. It has just occurred to me that I have often referred to 'we' and it might give the impression that we were always in the same group. Not so; whenever we were with a small group, the other members of the group were always people I had never seen before. We knew each other by our assumed names at these meetings and never saw each other again. The reason I stayed together with my roommate was because the plan was that we would be dropped together and we should get to know each other.

When in London, I had called the Dutch Merchant Navy office to inquire about Capt. Sissingh and was told that he was in a convalescent home for merchant navy personnel and was given his phone number. I had called him once in a while, but I never had the opportunity to go and see him and felt that now was the time to do just that, as I was to leave soon for Holland. So, one day when nothing was scheduled for the afternoon, I called and asked him if I could pay him a visit if that suited him. He was delighted and gave me the information about trains.

On meeting him, I realised that he had trouble walking and keeping his balance. After we sat down, he told me his story. He had been on the Murmansk run transporting military equipment destined for the Russian war effort when his ship was torpedoed off the northern coast of Norway in January, 1943. He and his crew had managed to board the lifeboats before his ship went down. It was bitterly cold and the Norwegian coast was within easy reach. But rather than falling into the hands of the Germans, he took command of the boats and headed towards Russia. It took them almost two weeks to reach Russia and during this time he and his crew suffered severe frostbite; Captain Sissingh had suffered severe frostbite and as a consequence had to have his toes amputated.

He had been awarded the DSM[4]. We spent a very pleasant afternoon as he told me everything he had done since he last saw his family. Of course I could not tell him that I was training to go back to Holland, and he had no idea that all he told me that afternoon would be told to his family in a matter of a few weeks.

---

[4] DSM – Distinguished Service Medal

Chapter Seven

Passed Ready for Action, Preparing to Drop into Holland

The final test to prove that I was ready for duty was to travel to Liverpool, in civilian clothes to make a report on the bottleneck in the harbour area and to recommend the best place and time for an enemy bombardment. In other words, I was to pose as a German spy and try not to get caught before my assignment was complete. I was given false identification papers in yet another name, some money, a suit of clothes and underwear, and off I went to Liverpool. I must make it clear that I was totally unaware that the office in London would be phoning the Liverpool police and warn them to be on the lookout for a German spy in the city. The next day, they intended to provide the police with a few more details: a rather tall chap with dark hair and darkish complexion. If I escaped detection to the end of the second day, they would then give my name, the colour of my suit, where they would likely find me, and other details to ensure my capture.

I decided that the very first thing the police would do to keep a check on possible spies in the region, would be to check all the hotels to see who had booked in during the last few days. Therefore, I decided to stay away from hotels and made a deal with the madam of a brothel that I could stay in one of her rooms. I explained to her that I did not want any of her 'services' but that I just wanted to have a place where I would not be disturbed for a few days. It must be recognized that, during the war, anybody of my age in civilian clothes, obviously not working and snooping around in the area of the railway lines in the port area would be very suspicious.

I probably did quite well since I was not apprehended until day four, when I was arrested and hauled to the police jail. The Chief of Police phoned London to report that they had their man, and was told that I would be picked up in a few days. In the meantime, the police were asked to interrogate me and to try to get as much information as possible from me. I was subjected to almost non-stop interrogation by different police officers with a constant bright light shining in my eyes. Once in a while they would haul me back to a cell in the basement. The cell had a concrete floor and was totally bare; the atmosphere was musty and felt as if it was used for drunks to sober up during the night. By halfway through the second day, I had managed to keep strictly to my initial story and the police officers were getting progressively more irritated at the prospect of not being able to tell the 'gentleman' from London, who would be collecting me, they had had any success in extracting information. Nothing incriminating had been found in my pockets because I never made notes and I always left my unfinished report under my mattress in the brothel, and they had not found out where I was staying.

When the man from London arrived, the police were told that I was one of their 'students' and he was keen to know how much information they had been able to get out of me. Naturally he was very pleased that they had been unsuccessful. I was brought up from my cell and received an apology for the rough treatment, and then congratulations on the successful completion of my assignment. It seems that I had passed with flying colours! I had scribbled notes for my report on the bottleneck(s) of the railways at or around the harbour on a piece of paper left under my mattress at the brothel, but I was able to write a detailed report from memory.

On the journey back to London, I was asked how I had managed to keep my assumed name from being traced by the police. They would soon have found it in the registry of one of the hotels, but they had not been able to find my name anywhere nor where I had been staying. When I told him, he burst out laughing, "That's a very novel idea, and how did you ever think of that?" I replied, "It was obvious to me that the first place to check would be to look in the hotel registers. I couldn't think of any other place where I could stay undetected, and for very little money to boot! They always gave me a friendly 'hello' when I came in and never asked any questions"!

My training was now finished and I would probably be scheduled to leave soon. I was asked to select the location where I would like to be dropped, which then had to be approved by the RAF (Royal Air Force). I could also choose if I wanted a reception committee. Since I had left Holland some ten months or so ago, I didn't feel that it was necessary and opted for a 'blind drop' with no one anticipating my arrival.

It was the beginning of May 1944; everyone knew that the invasion on mainland Europe was imminent. London, where a few months before one could see soldiers everywhere, was starting to empty. Everybody knew the reason: they had all been shipped to the southwest of England to get ready for the invasion. There were a very few people who knew when the invasion would be, but they were not talking. Everybody else just kept on guessing and every day there was a new date in the paper. My roommate now was Bert de Goede, who was going to be on my team. We were kept busy going over the codes again and fine-tuning our cover stories. Every time I reread my story I found some more holes that could have tripped me up.

One day someone from Head Quarters came to discuss the type of false papers I would need. Since I was likely to meet some people that I already knew in Holland, my false papers had to explain my prolonged absence to avoid any suspicions being raised. As a solution to this problem, I wanted to be a person who was working on a German ship, on two weeks leave in Holland. This meant that I had to have a piece of paper, that said so, and also a piece of paper stamped by the German Border Authorities, that would show that I had crossed the border. Since this would cover me for only a few weeks, I needed several of each document undated, which I would fill in myself before my 'leave' was up. I also needed a certificate from a Dutch doctor, declaring me fit for service in the navy, and dated before I went on my first job back in 1942, plus an official Dutch ID card that everybody was supposed to carry. After all these documents were printed I scrutinized them thoroughly to make sure that they would pass inspection. The forgers had done a masterful job and the papers looked very real, they were certainly good enough to fool any German in the west of Holland. However, I was not satisfied with the ID card. Before I left Holland, I had been involved in the distribution of false ID cards, and the underground had stolen quite a number of blanks. I knew that I could easily and quickly obtain an authentic ID card with my false name in Holland. I would have to use the unsatisfactory card in the meantime.

Finally, on June 6, 1944, the much postponed and long anticipated invasion of Normandy began. The location had been kept secret up until then and for a considerable period of time the Germans had been led to believe that the landings would take place further north in the Straits of Dover.[5] We were ready to go and became more anxious by the day, though we knew that we were waiting for the next moon period, for it is safer to drop on the darkest nights. While we waited I had to go to a dentist for a check-up. The dentist found a couple of cavities and proceeded to fill them, but he was careful to use exactly the same material as was used in Holland that differed from the materials used in England. Quite incredible attention to detail!

Some time in early June we were moved to a small hotel, on the north side, and overlooking Hyde Park. One evening we heard a strange 'put-put' sound and at the same time the sound of anti-aircraft fire. Looking out from our balcony we could see a low-flying object that looked like a small aircraft. 'What a brave pilot!' I thought, wondering how much longer it could last before it was shot down. It came right over us and then, a short while later, the engine noise stopped followed by an explosion. The next morning, the headlines in the paper read: 'Doodlebug explodes in London'. Other names for it included 'robot plane', and 'flying bomb'; we had witnessed the first V-1 fired at London. Eight thousand more were to follow but

---

[5] For details of deception operations suggest you read: 'Bodyguard of Lies' by Anthony Cave-Brown'

fortunately only two thousand reached their target. The ones that got through did a lot of damage, destroyed a large number of homes and killed almost six thousand people. The rockets were fired from permanent launching sites in Denmark, Holland, Belgium and France; carried a two thousand pound warhead, flew at an altitude of three to five thousand feet, and had a range of two hundred and fifty miles. Most of them were shot down or brought down while still over the Channel, others were downed by anti-aircraft fire over the land and others by colliding with chains hanging from helium filled balloons along the coastline. They did not have any guidance system but were simply sent aloft and pointed in the direction of London with just enough fuel to reach their target. Some fighter pilots even developed a manoeuvre whereby they would fly just below V-1 and then roll over creating a vacuum causing the rocket to veer off course and plunge into the ocean, without firing a single shot.

After the launching sites in France were destroyed by the advancing Allies, the target of choice changed to Antwerp in Belgium, the main Allied port. V-2s were developed soon after the V1s; they were launched mostly from mobile sites. In fact the V-2s were the first long range ballistic missiles with a trajectory that took them to almost twenty-five thousand feet before starting to descend. They were fired from hundreds of miles away from their intended target. There was no defence against the V-2 and no advanced warning. They were designed to explode on the slightest impact and the damage was caused mainly by the sideways blast of the explosions. I was in a square in London shortly after a V-2 had exploded and witnessed the wounded being carried out of a building. They had hardly any clothes on their bodies, their clothes had been torn to shreds by the fragments of glass from the windows, and they were covered with blood. There was no sign of a crater anywhere in the square. Before the war came to an end more than seventeen hundred of these had been launched. The V-2 was developed by Wernher von Braun, one of the worlds foremost rocket scientists. He and his group of engineers managed to sneak away and make their way to the front lines to surrender to the Allies. Soon after the war ended the Americans recruited almost the entire scientific team and von Braun later became a major player at NASA.

PART III:

Chapter Eight

Night Drop into Holland, Making Connections: 1944

On July 5, 1944, almost exactly a month after the Normandy invasion, word came that we would be jumping that night. We would be driven to the Tempsford airfield, about sixty kilometres due north of London.

My orders for action in Holland were:

- to contact, arm and train members of the underground organizations and to organize the activities of the resistance forces in Rotterdam;
- to arrange for drop zones to receive arms shipments and explosives;
- to organize the reception and distribution of these weapons and explosives and to train people how to use them;
- to report anything of military importance, in particular V1 and V2 launching sites, also the location of anti-aircraft installations and any troop movements.

Before leaving London, we were joined by a third person who was to be the wireless operator of our team. He introduced himself to us as 'Arnold'. In Tempsford we were dropped off at the 'barn'; on the outside it looked like a dilapidated wooden structure, but on the inside it had brick walls dividing it into three or four separate rooms[6]. We were each shown into one of the rooms that had all our gear laid out

---

[6] See photograph

ready. We carefully went over all the items to make sure that nothing was missing. It was mid-afternoon and we did not need to change into our civilian clothes and prepare ourselves until the early evening, until then we were free to do what we wanted.

There was some commotion outside and who should step into the barn but Prince Bernhard of the Netherlands, the son-in-law of Queen Wilhelmina, dressed in RAF uniform. The Prince had his office in London on the floor above Kas de Graaf's office and on occasion we had met him in the elevator. He visited the general and also de Graaf occasionally, and was obviously quite well informed about events. I knew that the prince flew for the R.A.F. as a fighter pilot and that he had false identification papers when he was on a mission, in case he was shot down and ended up in German hands. He came towards us and shook hands. "I am here to see you fellows off" he said, "I like to do this if I get a chance". He suggested that we go to the mess for a drink. Here we spent the next hour chatting with the prince who appeared to be very interested in our mission and questioned us extensively about it. When he left, he shook hands with each of us once more and wished us success with our mission.

After a meal it was time to prepare ourselves for the drop. We each went to our own cubicle where they had laid out all our clothes: underwear, shoes, socks, suit, shirt and tie. When I examined the shoes, I noticed that there was no brand name on them, but the suit had the name of a Dutch tailor in Rotterdam on the inside of the jacket and the underwear too was a Dutch brand. Again, incredible attention had been made to every detail! Last, but of extreme importance was the stack of micro-prints with five letter groups, our coding- and decoding silk, a supply of Benzedrine pills, and one rubber-coated suicide capsule. The latter was meant to be held in your mouth if you landed in a situation where there was no way out. You could keep the uncrushed pill in your mouth as long as necessary; crushed and death would occur in less than ten seconds.

I had finished getting ready, when we were asked to check our pockets one last time. I had already done that, but when I emptied my wallet again and checked the contents I was embarrassed to find a halfpenny coin mixed in with the Dutch coins! While in England, I had got used to carrying all my change in my pants pocket. This is not customary in Holland, so I had put my loose coins in my wallet but I had missed the halfpenny. We each carried a Colt32, which we carried in our pockets, in case we needed a weapon upon landing. As there was still quite a bit of time before we were to board the plane, we went to the lounge again for a coffee and to catch the latest news about the invasion. The Allies by then appeared to have control of a fairly large area surrounding the landing beaches and had not experienced excessive resistance. Just after midnight we were told to don our parachutes and get ready to board.

Finally! The moment I had been waiting for, for such a long time! We walked across the airfield in the bright moonlit and were climbed into the plane, a Hudson, in which we were to be flown across to Holland. In the dim light inside I saw what looked like a slide in the floor of the fuselage, instead of a hole. We were to straddle the slide, sitting one behind the other. Behind the last person, also on the slide, was a large package with our equipment: radios, transmitters, and explosives. The door was closed and the plane took off. There were the three of us and a dispatcher who was busy attaching our rigging lines to the plane.

As we passed over one of the islands in the northwest of Holland we heard some anti-aircraft fire and could see tracer bullets streaking through the dark. Soon we felt the plane losing altitude and shortly thereafter the red light came on in front of us. This light indicated 'action stations'. The dispatcher opened the hatch in the floor at the end of the 'slide' we were sitting on, the red light changed to green, and down the hatch we went followed by the package with the rest of our equipment. As we descended, we could see each other clearly in the moonlit sky. The plane maintained the same course and disappeared in the dark. We were on the ground within a few seconds. Arnold and I, and the parcel, landed in a grain field. Bert, unfortunately, landed in the trees at the edge of the field, and we found him hanging about eight feet above the ground. We managed to jump up and grab him by the ankles that caused the branches to break and bring Bert and his parachute down. Fortunately, he had not unlatched himself from his parachute, otherwise we would have had to climb the tree to free and retrieve it.

There was a lot work ahead of us before we could leave the area. Four parachutes, the parcel with our equipment, and our jump suits all had to be buried, and also the three shovels we had used to dig the holes. We buried everything in the woods close to the edge of the grain field; we were lucky because the soil was fairly sandy and the digging relatively easy. This also made it easier to fill in the holes to make it look undisturbed; we even planted most of the weeds that we had carefully set aside before we started digging. This all took over an hour but since it was still dark we decided to stay put until daylight so that we could inspect the site to make sure that nothing looked suspicious. After the war ended about ten months later, Boy and Josh went back to the spot where we had buried everything and managed to find the parachutes still intact. But the duffel bag we had stuffed the chutes into had completely disintegrated. The chutes were immediately claimed by the ladies who used the silk to make blouses and underwear for themselves and their daughters. They had not seen material like that for a long time!

From this day forward until the end of the war my name was to be:
L.G. Dijkerman

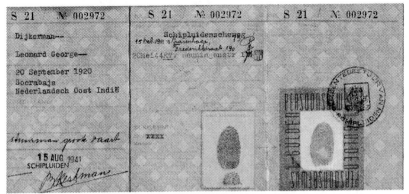

Front and back of ID

My cover story was that I was employed on the S.S. 'Ceuta' of the Oldenburg-Portugiesische Dampschiffs- Rhederei in Hamburg, on sick leave from August 29 to October 15,1944.

Oldenburg-Portugiesische Dampfschiffs-Rhederei

Fernsprecher :
32 18 91 / 94

Bankkonto :
Deutsche Bank
Filiale Hamburg

Dresdner Bank
in Hamburg

Postscheckkonto :
Hamburg Nr. 250.99

Fernschreib-Nr.
02—1110

Li/K   Hamburg 1, am   27 August 1944
Mönckebergstr. 27

B E S C H E I N I G U N G.

Der Leonard George D i j k e r m a n ist bei der
Besatzung dés Dampfers "Ceuta" als 3. Offz.
eingesetzt.

Er hat Erholungsurlaub vom 29. August bis zum
15. Okt. 1944. Sein Seefahrtsbuch wird von der
Heuerstelle der Firma zurückgehalten.

I needed several documents to be able to travel
and verify my story.

In order to cross the border into Holland I was
issued with a border-crossing pass which was valid for
only one return trip.

The documents were made out for the period of
August 29 to October 15, 1944. I was also issued with
extra documents for the periods of October 16 to
December 1 and for a few additional six-week periods
which would have carried me through until the end of
the war.

90

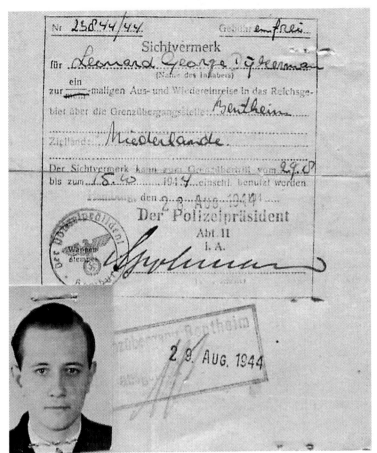

Border Crossing Pass

It was necessary for me to establish my 'history'. For this purpose I was provided with a discharge certificate from the S.S. Norden (also a German boat) showing that I had worked there from December 12, 1942 till October 18, 1943, and Certificates of Health, dated January 6, 1941 and November 10, 1941.

I was issued with two food distribution cards, one dated October 15, 1941 and a second undated card.

So, if a stranger were to examine these papers it would most certainly establish the fact that I, L.G. Dijkerman, was a legitimate citizen.

The fact that I had been working for German shipping companies also gave the impression that I was sympathetic to the Germans.

All the false documents were produced by MI5 or MI6 and they did a superb job indeed. They all looked as if I'd had them for quite a while, some of them folded and in my pocket for a while. The paper on the older ones had even yellowed a bit.

The rest of the night was completely silent and the moon was still shining bright. Although we had not slept for almost twenty-four hours, none of us felt sleepy. I lit a cigarette and sat down on the ground feeling completely relaxed. We began to discuss our plan of action. We decided we would leave the area and go south. Since I had picked the spot to be dropped, I assumed that we were a few kilometres north of the town of Epe. We planned to leave one at a time, about ten minutes apart. The aim was that we should still be close enough to able to see each other and yet not appear to be members of the same group. We had seen farm buildings to the south of us and assumed that there would be a road from the farm to the nearest town.

As dawn broke, we thoroughly inspected the area and inconspicuously marked the spot where we had buried our equipment. We all needed to know this location because one of us would have to return soon to dig up the equipment needed. I was the first to leave and headed towards the farm. As I had expected, I came upon a road and when I had followed it for a short distance I could see a town in the distance. It was still only five o'clock and I calculated that I should reach the town at about seven o'clock, if I walked slowly. I looked back and saw Arnold, the second one to leave, in the distance. The sun had come up and it was a beautiful summer morning; so still and peaceful. The air smelled fresh. It was hard to imagine that there was a war raging on further to the south in France. I came to a crossroads and a sign, 'Epe 2 km', pointed in the direction I was going. Everything was going as planned; the pilot had dropped us at the precise spot that I had selected. England now seemed to be so far away and such a long time ago!

When I reached Epe, there was a bus stop across the road and I walked over and read the sign: 'Apeldoorn'. It was precisely where I wanted to go to catch a train to Rotterdam. The next bus was due in about twenty minutes, leaving plenty of time for Arnold to get there. I sat down on the bench and lit a cigarette. I had a cigarette holder with unmarked cigarettes but the smell of the tobacco smoke was unmistakably that of British cigarettes so I had to be careful and not smoke these in a public place. A Dutchman approached the bench with a 'Good morning' and sat down; I had seen him coming and quickly extinguished my cigarette.

'Going to Apeldoorn?' he asked.

'Yes, catching the train to Arnhem'.

He nodded, pulled a newspaper out of his pocket to read. Soon after, a German soldier joined us with a 'Gute Morgen!' rather than the usual: 'Heil Hitler!' I mumbled a 'morn' but the other Dutchman kept silent. The soldier was an older man and therefore unlikely to be a Nazi. His friendly greeting was further evidence of this. A few minutes later, Arnold came walking towards the bench and I noticed his uneasiness at the sight of the German soldier; he put his right hand into his overcoat pocket where I knew he had his pistol. When he looked at me, I shook my head and motioned him to sit down with a 'Good morning!' in Dutch of course. Instead of answering me in Dutch, he mumbled a distinctly English: 'Mornin'. When he realized his mistake, his face turned red. However, neither the Dutchman nor the German soldier paid the slightest attention. I realized that this was the first time Arnold had seen a German soldier because he had been a sailor on a cargo ship when Germany invaded Holland and had not been back to Holland since. The bus arrived and Arnold and I sat down beside each other. There were three more German soldiers on the bus. I whispered to Arnold to take his hand out of his pocket and he reluctantly did so. He obviously felt very uneasy and probably expected that he would have to shoot his way out of this situation any time soon.

Before boarding the bus we had seen Bert a few hundred meters from the edge of town. He was to stay with a friend in Epe and knew how to contact me later. I had given him a friend's phone number, at which he was to leave a message with a phone number at which he could be reached. That is if everything was OK! If not he was to give my friend a different message and no phone number. If he had not called within ten days, I would know that he was in serious trouble.

The bus to Apeldoorn, very conveniently, took us right to the train station. Arnold and I each bought a ticket to Rotterdam via Arnhem, where we had to change trains. There were lots of German soldiers on the train and I was relieved to notice that Arnold seemed to be increasingly at ease with them. Even a slip of the tongue he made, 'Oh, I am sorry!' didn't seem to upset him much. However, I cautioned him to be very careful because such slip-ups could result in an ID check and perhaps even a body search resulting in the discovery of his gun. Personally, I was very uncomfortable having a gun on me and planned to put it away as soon as possible after arriving in Rotterdam.

The train trip to Rotterdam was uneventful. The station had not been bombed but when we left the station, I saw again the devastation of the 1940 bombardment. The entire area that used to be Rotterdam's shopping area of was flattened. This time, I no longer felt helpless, and it made me more determined than ever to do everything possible to help the Allies defeat the Germans. Arnold and I took the streetcar to Hillegersberg. I was looking forward to arriving at the Sissinghs' home and seeing the surprised looks on their faces. They had probably assumed that I was gone for the duration of the war. It was ten months since I had left and as far as all my friends in Rotterdam were concerned, I was either in Sweden or, possibly, in England. We walked from the tram stop to the little park at the lake and sat on a bench for a while, just to make sure that nobody had followed us. Nobody else was on the beach apart from a few mothers with their children. We sat for about half an hour watching the children playing and set off for the Sissingh's house and I rang the doorbell.

Mrs. Sissingh opened the door and when she saw me, her mouth fell open, tears came into her eyes and she put her arms around me. Then she called, 'Boy, look who is here!' Boy came down and when he saw me, he just stared at me for a while, and then said,

'I don't believe it, is this real?

'Yes, it's me for real!'

We shook hands for a long time. I think we both wanted to let the significance of this event really sink in. Even though I had been preparing myself for the past six or seven months, it now felt to me like nothing short of a miracle!

I introduced them both to Arnold, who had been standing behind me all this time, and told Boy that I wanted to get accommodation for him as soon as possible, preferably today. Boy immediately went to phone someone who came an hour later to pick up Arnold to take him to his new temporary abode. It was just like old times again being there. We discussed my situation and decided that I should stay for a few days so that I could discuss my plans with Boy and the key people in his resistance group. While mother Sissingh was busily cooking dinner, Boy and I enjoyed a few beers and I told him about my experiences during the past months. I was very anxious to learn what progress had been made by the resistance groups in Holland while I was gone. Boy told me there were now several well-organized groups in Rotterdam as well as in the rest of Holland. There had been a few casualties here and there, but nothing major. I explained to him that I wanted to have a meeting with the key people of these various groups as soon as possible. I impressed on him the importance of maintaining the utmost security when organizing these meetings, and not to tell anyone who I was or where I came from. I myself planned to tell them that I was able to act as a contact between them and the person who was able to get messages to the Allies. I told Boy what type of weapons could be made available to them, and that each group should prepare a list of what would be required to fully arm their men.

Then, Boy's sisters, Beth and Jannie came home; when they entered the living room and saw me, their mouths fell open and Beth let out a loud scream. They both thought that I had come back from Sweden. I waited until after dinner before telling them about their father in London. They were saddened by the fact that he was now crippled but on the other hand glad that he was no longer at sea, plying the waters of the North Atlantic and the Barents Sea. I told them what had happened to me in the past ten months and why I was here. I sensed immediately that Beth did not want to have anything to do with this type of activity. But Jannie's eyes lit up and she started to ask questions; Boy had already got her involved doing some courier work. She saw this as a great opportunity for the resistance groups in Rotterdam, as they would be able to communicate soon with our Allies across the water.

When Mrs. Sissingh and Beth had gone to bed, the three of us talked till the early hours in the morning. Jannie was to continue her role as a courier. We drew up a plan to pick up Bert and the equipment buried at the edge of the woods. Boy knew a policeman who had a permit to drive a car and suggested that they would drive to Epe to pick up Bert, who would then guide them to the spot where our equipment was buried. The policeman would then take our equipment to Rotterdam with Boy handcuffed in the backseat. In the event that they were stopped at a German checkpoint on their way back, they would have a perfect excuse for being on the road. Bert would then travel by train to Rotterdam a couple of days later.

The next afternoon Bert called me to let me know where he was and I explained our plan to him. I would let him know when he could expect Boy and the policeman, and I suggested that he stay in Epe a few more days to give us time to get things organized and that I would call him when we were ready. By that time I would have been able to find a safe place for him to stay.

I spent the next morning walking around the village and in the area around the lakes. It was obvious that the war had taken a toll on the population; there was little laughter and everyone was preoccupied with food. I saw that the store shelves were getting empty and everyone's shoes and clothes had started to look worn. I went into a shoe store, and noticed that most of the shoes had been labelled 'composition soles'. When I asked the clerk the soles were made of, he replied, 'mostly impregnated cardboard with thin leather on the very bottom'. He added, 'They usually don't last more than six months, most of the good sole leather is now being shipped to Germany'.

There were very few young people left in Holland. If you were less than thirty years old and did not have an essential occupation, you would soon be on your way to a forced labour camp in Germany. The ones that had managed to stay had a pass that stated that they were either physically unfit or that they were employed in some essential industry in Holland; essential to the Germans of course! These people were either directly or indirectly working for the occupation force. The more stamps, in particular German stamps, you had on your pass, the better the chance that you would not be shipped off to Germany. I felt pretty safe with my piece of paper that said that I was second officer on a German ship on two weeks leave, and another piece of paper that indicated that I had crossed the border at Bentheim in the north-east of Holland a couple of days ago. I almost started to believe it myself!

At this time of year the lakes were usually brimming with activity, but now I saw very few boats. In the afternoon I called Peter de Beer (White Pete), who also lived in Hillegersberg, and asked him if we could meet somewhere. I had known him ever since my first holiday at Christmas in 1939, and I knew that he was in Boy's group. He seemed to be a bit surprised at hearing my voice but didn't ask any questions. We had been involved with the distribution of food coupons to the Jewish families before I left Holland, and I knew that Peter had also been involved with the theft of hundreds of blank ID cards and had a contact in the ID office. This contact would later officially enter the number and, usually false, name on the ID in the registry. I have always felt that Peter's main asset was his very innocent and always smiling baby face. I didn't think anybody would ever suspect him of doing anything he was not supposed to do. But beneath that innocent face he was as hard as a rock and totally fearless.

When we met, he asked, 'I don't suppose that you have come back from Sweden? 'No, I certainly didn't', and I told him my story. He pledged his full support and later became one of the most active and daring of all the people with whom I worked. I could always count on him. His actions were very calculated; he was a quick thinker, never reckless, and nothing seemed to faze him, he always seemed to have a solution to any problem. Later that day I called Josh, who was also a frequent visitor to the Sissingh family and had been ever since I got to know him before our boat holiday in 1940. He was another person one could always count on, cut from the same cloth as White Pete. Josh's particular strength was as a master planner, he undertook any task without fear, but always considered and planned for the dangers involved. Josh and I met at a small park along the lake; like Peter, he sensed that I had not returned from Sweden but did not ask for details. When I explained to him why I had come back to Holland he immediately pledged his full support.

I spent the next few days meeting with Boy, Josh and Pete. We made plans for the future; Boy had got in touch with his friend, the policeman, who had agreed to do whatever was necessary but suggested that it would be safer to go with two policemen. He also intended to arrange for an arrest warrant for Boy to make it look totally legitimate. It would take a few days before he would be ready to go. Arnold was going to need a place where he could set up his transmitter, preferably not the address at which he was staying, as this would compromise the other people in the house. For this very same reason I also needed a place where I could safely stay, because being in the same house as Boy would not be good for either of us. Josh would spend the next few days looking for a place for the transmitter. Pete, in the meantime, was going to contact the leaders of the resistance groups in Rotterdam and set up dates and places for me to meet them.

Three days later the policemen phoned to tell us that they were ready to go the next day and arranged to pick up Boy early in the morning. Everything went as planned and they were back, having recovered all of our buried equipment, the same day. They had not had any problem finding the spot where it was buried. All the items were now safely stored in their personal lockers at the police station. The equipment included two transmitters concealed in two small innocent looking suitcases[7], four small receivers, each about five by eight by twenty-four centimetres, and four batteries that were about the same size as the receivers. They were quite large compared to modern resistor type transmitters and receivers, but at that time, when tubes were still being used, they were electronic marvels. The tiny tubes were about the size of a thimble maybe even smaller. We only had to find a suitable place to set up the transmitter, and we would be "in business". Josh took Arnold with him to look for such a place so that Arnold could get familiar with the city and, at the same time, help Josh find a suitable place. They were in luck; two days later they found an ideal place, the attic of a Catholic church in the harbour area! The priest himself was involved in the underground movement and was known to Pete. He lived next door to the church in the manse that was connected to the back of the church. Arnold could go into the church and, if nobody was following him, slip through the back door and get the priest to open the door to the attic. Alternatively, he could go directly to the manse and enter the church through the back door.

---

[7] see picture

Josh had also found a suitable place for me. I went to meet the family, who had two young children. I thought that it was only fair to tell them that I was a member of the resistance and that there was a risk involved if they let me stay with them. They fully realized that there was a risk but were quite prepared to take it. I explained that I would probably get a visit on a regular basis from a young lady, who would bring me messages and asked them if they would be kind enough to let her in and allow her stay as long as necessary. They did not see that as a problem at all and I moved in that same day. I also wanted two additional addresses that I could use in the event of an emergency; ideally, suites with a separate entrance.

We had found a safe place for Bert and it was arranged that he would leave Epe for Rotterdam the next day. He also told me that he knew a girl in Epe, named Didi, who had done some courier work for him and other members of the resistance and who would like to come to Rotterdam to act as the courier for the three of us. We needed a courier, so it was agreed that she would travel with Bert. I told him they would be met by Josh who would take them to their respective living places. Josh had bought a second hand bicycle for both of them that would be waiting for them on arrival. He would show them the way to the little park by the lake where I would be waiting for them. I suggested that they should bring their bathing suits to make it look as innocent as possible. We would be able to talk quietly without raising suspicion.

When I called Boy later that evening and told him about our planned meeting at the beach, he commented that it was a novel idea, and in fact, we could set up most of our meetings that way! I said that we would need a set of large-scale army maps showing latitude and longitude, and landmarks; we would need these to be able to pinpoint the locations of the drop zones. Boy thought that he might know a person who would know how to obtain such maps. When I saw him the next day, he was smiling from ear to ear and showed me a metal army-green box with a set of very detailed army maps of Holland. I was delighted with them; it was just what we needed! We only needed one or two maps at a time when we start pinpointing the drop zones and could leave the rest at home. Boy said he had got them from the person for whom I had carried messages to Sweden. He happened to have two sets and was very willing to part with one of them. He was ecstatic when he learned to whom they were being given, and how they were going to be used.

The next day I went to the train station with Josh to meet Bert and Didi, the girl from Epe who was to act as our courier. When I spotted Bert in the crowd I pointed him out to Josh and then I left and took the tram to Hillegersberg. Since I had plenty of time, I had a cup of coffee in the village before going to the park at the lake. When I got there I saw that Bert and Didi had already arrived and changed into their bathing suits; they looked like a perfectly innocent couple. I sat on a bench for a while and looked around to check that I was not being followed. We had the whole place to ourselves, so I strolled over to Bert who introduced me to Didi. She seemed to be a very nice girl and gave me the impression that she was very keen and capable. I explained to her that she would be the courier between Bert, Arnold and me. However, if she met somebody here who knew that she had been acting as a courier before, I would like her to give that person some reason that she was no longer involved, as an extra precaution. I then explained to her who we were and she would be carrying coded messages between the three of us as soon as Arnold had his transmitter set up. I promised her that I would arrange for her to meet Arnold soon and suggested that, in the meantime, she should acquaint herself with Rotterdam and our respective living places. She had already met the people with whom Bert was staying and I told her that I would also introduce her to the family with whom I was staying.

The official part of our meeting completed we could now enjoy the picnic lunch Mrs. Sissingh had prepared for us, and we spent the rest of the afternoon loafing on the beach and swimming in the lake. After all, what better way to spend a beautiful summer afternoon? In these peaceful surroundings war seemed to be far away. At the same time we were constantly aware of the fact that we were in a hostile environment and had to be always on guard. I say 'we' because everybody in the underground felt the same way. Everything had to be carefully planned; if something went wrong there had to be a way out and we always made sure that we were not being followed. After four years of war and working in the underground it had become a way of life. And yet, there were still casualties, often involving more than just one person. That is why it was so important to keep personal contact to a minimum, not to make any notes of names and phone numbers, and not to know anything that was unnecessary. Gossip was our biggest enemy. All our meetings took place after taking every possible security precaution. This would often involve such ruses as leading anyone who might be tracking us on a wild goose chase by first going window-shopping or going into stores. Once we decided that we were not being followed, and finally did meet, we always pretended that it was a chance meeting and acted accordingly.

A few days after this meeting in the park, I wrote my first message to London and coded it. It read: 'All OK, contacts made. ID cards bad'. I felt that I should let them know that the ID cards we were given in England were not satisfactory. It was now almost three weeks since we had been dropped and I surmised that by now they must be quite anxious to hear from us. I phoned Arnold and asked him when he would be ready for his first scheduled transmission. Fortunately, he had set up his equipment that afternoon and checked it out and was ready to transmit the next afternoon. I promised him that he would have my first message in his hands by then. The transmission times given to all wireless operators in the field were always different and of very short duration, just long enough to establish contact, send the message, and sign off. These periods were often changed by way of coded messages broadcast by the BBC; radio frequencies used were also changed on a regular basis. The German intelligence had numerous 'DF (direction finders) units' concealed inside innocent looking vans with fictitious business names. The vans would converge on the location of the transmitter as soon as they picked up a transmission. The shorter the period on the air, the less chance you had that the units would pick you up and get close enough to become a threat. But once they picked you up, they knew one of the frequencies that would then be constantly monitored by a stationary receiver. We had been given three different frequencies that we could use at random at all our skeds (scheduled transmission times). However, this meant that once the Germans had picked you up on all the frequencies they would be monitoring us on a twenty-four hour basis. Hence, as soon as we found a location for our second transmitter we would be in a better position to elude detection. That night we received a response from London; they had indeed been concerned and hoped to hear from us again soon.

Chapter Nine

Urgent Need for Supplies, Organizing Air Drops

Boy and Pete had by now arranged meetings with the leaders of the resistance groups in Rotterdam and other cities in Holland. Three or four exhausting weeks were spent traveling all over Holland to meet the leaders. It often entailed staying awake for long periods of time and on one occasion I had to use Benzedrine, known as 'stay awake pills', which I had been issued in England. Once, I managed to stay awake for seventy-two hours, when I finally had the opportunity to go to sleep I was surprised to wake up ten hours later feeling as fit as a fiddle.

During these meetings the leaders all expressed their concern about the lack of weapons, without which only minor acts of sabotage were possible. Also such acts of sabotage against the Germans quite often resulted in innocent people being arrested and sometimes publicly executed. The leaders were ecstatic when I assured them that the supply of weapons to the resistance movement was my first priority. I explained in detail to each group what was required to make the delivery of weapons a reality. They had to pinpoint suitable locations for weapons drops and, after ensuring the complete cooperation of the landowner, to provide me with the exact longitude and latitude of the selected location. Also, before deciding on a location, they should scout the surrounding areas for anti-aircraft batteries and searchlights and try to determine if there was a way for a pilot to avoid these when making a drop. In addition, the groups should make a note of, and if possible pinpoint the location of enemy installations such as V1 and V2 launching sites. Such launching sites should be reported immediately because the V2s were launched from a trailer and were thus highly mobile and never left in one location for long.

Thorough and proper homework was essential because the locations would all be scrutinized by the RAF before any further action was taken; if sites were not approved, much work would be for naught. I gave each group leader the sections of the map of the area they would be scouting; they covered a large area in between and around the cities of Amsterdam, The Hague, Rotterdam, and Utrecht. Once a group had delivered the location of a suitable dropping site, they would receive further instructions on how and when to proceed. During this period, Bert had also been meeting with resistance leaders in other parts of the country to try to set up a network of locations suitable for arms drops. It became very clear that there was a lot of work that had to done before any weapons would come falling from the sky.

However, proposed drop sites started coming and Bert and I, were kept busy coding the messages, and Arnold transmitting them to London for approval. Arnold was so busy in fact that I decided to turn over most of the transmitting concerning drop sites to Bert, and Bert kept me posted about the approved locations and the group involved with specific locations. Bert stayed mostly in Rotterdam in close contact with Arnold, and I travelled all over Holland to instruct the leaders of the reception teams on the proper procedure to follow to guide the pilots and to identify themselves to the pilots. When the first reports came in we sent the locations to the RAF for approval. Bert and I each had a micro-photograph, the size of a postage stamp with all the information pertaining to the drop locations. The first column was the code name, followed by a recognition letter to be signalled in Morse code with a flashlight to the pilot on approach of the field, and the last column contained a short sentence. Every evening at eight o'clock, and again at ten, the BBC would broadcast a number of these sentences. If the message pertained to your location, it meant that the drop was going to take place during that night. As soon as we received word from London that a particular location was approved, we would tell the group involved and tell them which sentence to listen for. At the same time we would give them the recognition signal for the approaching aircraft. From that time on they were to listen to the BBC every night at eight and ten. If their sentence was read they should alert their team and get ready to receive the arms drop. I wanted to be at the first drop, just to make sure that everything went as planned so I asked the group concerned to keep me informed of their preparations. Each drop usually consisted of twenty-four containers of about 200 lbs each all of which had to be moved into safe storage before daylight. Also, twenty-four parachutes had to be buried. Although only three or four men were required before and during the drop, as soon as all the containers were on the ground many more men were needed.

It became obvious quite quickly that we needed another wireless operator, and at least a few additional transmitters. The more locations we had to transmit from the less chance there was of being detected. I composed a second telegram requesting London to send additional transmitters as soon as possible, also a shipment of four containers with a few hundred small handguns, explosives and other sabotage materials.

At this time I received word from one of the resistance groups that they were hiding three US airmen who had bailed out when their aircraft was shot down over Holland; this necessitated a third telegram to ask for further directions. We received a response from London the following day; they had indeed been concerned and hoped to hear from us again soon. They also wanted to know what was wrong with the ID cards. London gave us a phone number and password so we could get in touch with a member of the 'Pilot Escape Line', which led to me meeting Jimmy, one of the US airmen who was supposed to act as a 'deaf and dumb' when out and about. One day, I spotted him in town happily whistling a popular Benny Goodman tune! I hurried over, gave him a poke in the ribs, and told him not to whistle. He gave me a surprised look and said: 'Why? I am not supposed to hear or speak but I can sure whistle!' I responded that if he could not hear, how could he possibly know the tune? He smiled and said: 'OK'.

Several drop sites were rejected but eventually several were approved by the beginning of August and we were expecting to receive several drops during the moon period during the first half of August. From now on we had to listen to the BBC news every night to find if a drop was planned for that night. Each night we listened anxiously to the BBC but no messages came. Finally a telegram came from London to say that due to bad weather and low cloud cover, all shipments during the period had had to be cancelled. The next drops would be planned to take place in a couple of weeks.

As scheduled, the first message came through on August 28. I immediately phoned the person responsible for the site identified, to make sure that he had heard the message and that his crew would be in place and ready. He assured me that they were well prepared and would be on location just as soon as he could contact them. The leader of the reception group called the next day to tell me that he had received the 'potatoes' that he had ordered and that he was happy with the good quality. He asked me when I would have the next shipment ready and I told him to let me know as soon as his stock was getting low!

The approved location was close to Rotterdam, and I decided to lead the reception team for the first drop. I met the group, told them to listen to the BBC every night, and to go to the site as soon as the message for this drop was broadcast. I only needed three people to guide the plane in and instructed the others to stay out of sight and only come onto the field after the drop had been made. It could be dangerous to be on the field during the drop as the two hundred pound containers were dropped from a very low altitude and close together so it could be a problem to get out the way!

A few days later the message for this site close to Rotterdam came through on the BBC. Jannie had been pestering me to allow her to help and I had finally broken down. When I heard the message, I gave her a call and told her that I would be at her house shortly to pick her up. We bicycled to the location less than five kilometres from Rotterdam. It was a beautiful, clear, moonlit night and no sound was heard except for the distant and, by now, familiar drone of bombers on their way to Germany. When we arrived at the farm we went straight to the barn where a few others had already arrived ahead of us. It was close to eleven and I decided that the four of us needed should go to the field to guide the plane in. The others were to stay in the barn for ten minutes after the plane had come over making sure that everything was safe before coming onto the field. A final check of our flashlights and the four of us left.

Three of the group stood in a straight line about one hundred meters apart and I went off at a ninety degree angle and about twenty meters from the end of the line. Shortly after midnight we could hear the sound of a low flying aircraft in the distance. As it seemed to be getting closer, I gave the other three a signal with my flashlight to turn their flashlights on and I gave the identification signal assigned for this particular site: one long and two short for the letter 'D'. The sound of the aircraft grew ever louder and it appeared to be coming straight for us. Then it was overhead and we could see the dark silhouettes of the parachutes, with the cigar shaped containers underneath against the moonlit sky. Within seconds the containers were on the ground and the sound of the plane faded into the distance. I was overwhelmed by a feeling of immense pride and almost disbelief that we could have accomplished this feat undetected by the enemy all around us.

Yet, just a few weeks later, drops had become almost routine in all parts of Holland; every night when the moon was out, dozens of drops took place in every part of the country. Groups of agents were parachuted into different parts of Holland; establishing their own dropping sites with the local resistance groups and teaching them the use of the weapons and explosives. By the end of the war a total of two hundred and eleven drops had taken place delivering a staggering forty thousand pounds of explosives, more than twenty thousand sten-guns; a combined total of more than nine thousand bren-guns, rifles, carbines, pistols, bazookas, and more than thirty-two thousand grenades.

But to return to our mission on that night, we remained immobile for at least ten minutes to make sure that everything was safe. I could see twenty parachutes on the ground, all within about a two hundred feet radius. The other men in the team started coming onto the field. I told them to first detach all the chutes from the containers, gather all the chutes together and move the containers to one spot close to the barn. I gave Jannie the responsibility of bundling the chutes and moving them into the barn. By two a.m. all the containers were gathered in one spot and we had checked the whole field to make sure that nothing had been left behind. As soon as it was daylight the farmer would hitch his rake behind a couple of horses and erase any evidence of our activities.

Our task was now to empty the containers, carry everything into the barn, and get rid of the containers and the parachutes. The farmer had suggested sinking the containers end for end into a drainage ditch that was about three feet deep and always at least two thirds full of water during the coming winter and spring months. This we did since the alternative was to either hide them underneath a haystack or bury them in the field, which would have been a huge and time consuming job. Hiding them underneath the hay was not a good option either because that was probably the first place the Germans would look if there were ever to be an investigation. By about three-thirty we had done everything including burying the bundle of parachutes. We gathered in the barn for a smoke and a rest; everybody was in high spirits. The farmer also came and joined in on our discussion; he wanted to know how we intended to transport everything to Rotterdam. No one had thought of a satisfactory solution so far, and we were all interested when the farmer suggested his old milk truck, that he was no longer using, might be suitable. The motor still ran well and we could build a small compartment in the back of the tank connected to the spigot and that could be filled with milk. He told us that the Germans at the checkpoint usually check the milk trucks before being allowed to proceed by cracking open the valve to ascertain that milk was in the tank. This was an excellent solution to the problem, and fortunately one member of our group had a friend with a welding shop who could easily build a small tank and do the necessary piping. The farmer said that he would drive the truck to the garage to get the engine checked over, and to have the springs reinforced because the loads would be considerably heavier than milk.

At this point I decided to go home not wanting to get involved with the details and feeling that all members of the group were well qualified to handle the transportation of the weapons into Rotterdam. I had brought a couple of small sacks with me and asked the farmer if he could sell me some potatoes to provide me with an alibi. That was no problem; and he filled both sacks and Jannie and I tied them onto our carriers; we paid for the potatoes and left. Jannie and I followed a country road on top of a dike and when we came close to Rotterdam we saw a small hut at the foot of the dike and a couple of men nearby. As we came closer we could see that they were German soldiers and that the hut was a sentry post that we had not seen in the dark the night before. One of the Germans came to the road and ordered us to stop.

'What are you doing here so early in the morning?' he asked.

'Getting some potatoes at the farm' was my response, pointing at the sack of my carrier.

He started to feel around the sacks and then stuck his knife in one of the bags. This made me angry and I told him that this was good food and that if he wanted to check the contents of the bags we would have opened them for him. He didn't answer but gave me a dirty look. The soldier then asked his partner whether he thought that they should investigate further and it looked as if he was going to order us to come down to the hut. I felt quite safe with my ID and papers from the German shipping company and there should be no problem for Jannie. But when I looked at her she suddenly turned red, she seemed nervous and started to flirt with the soldier. She was usually always very calm and in control, so this puzzled me. Her flirting apparently changed the German's mind and he told us that we could proceed. I said: 'Thank you' and Jannie gave him a big smile whereupon the soldier said that maybe they could meet each other some time.

We had gone a short distance, when I asked her: 'Why were you so nervous at the check point?' Jannie turned red again. 'I have to confess something! I know that I shouldn't have done it and I am very sorry. I promise never to do it again. I have a parachute stuffed in my jacket!' I was furious! She knew that this was against all rules and the consequences, if they had found it on her would have been disastrous. I told her that I was very disappointed and that I could not understand how she could do such an utterly stupid thing. She said again and again that she was sorry and that she just could not resist taking one parachute home for the material.

At that moment I realized that she had not seen the colour of the chutes in the dark, but I had had a glimpse of them in the light of my flashlight and they were all a dark orange. I started to laugh and she gave me a puzzled look as if to say: 'What are you laughing about?' I told her I was trying to visualize what she was going to look like in dark orange underwear. She commented that that would be her punishment, wearing dark orange underwear! We both laughed and never talked about the incident again. Nylon was unknown in Holland during the war and I later learned that it was a very difficult material to sew.

I learned a few weeks later that the milk truck had successfully completed several trips into Rotterdam and was being used to haul loads of weapons from other fields into Rotterdam. The driver of the truck had become very popular with the German sentries at the entrance of Rotterdam because rather than taking a small sample of the milk, he encouraged them to fill up their containers. Consequently, he had no trouble entering Rotterdam to deliver his load!

I needed a completely soundproof space where we could use live ammunition to be able to properly train the men. We had such a space built in the basement of a large house and tested to check if it was soundproof. The men inside would fire several short bursts with their sten-guns as we walked around the house outside to check for any sound. It was perfect, not a sound could be heard. I arranged with each group leader to call me as soon as his group was inside and he had checked that all was safe in the neighbourhood. Everybody needed earmuffs; everyone had to make their own as they were not available anywhere. There were no activities that required wearing earmuffs: no leaf blowers, power mowers, weed eaters, or power tools of any kind at that time. Each group left their muffs behind so that they could be used by the next group of trainees and as they were passed on from one to the other additional padding was added on to make them more soundproof. After a while all the earmuffs seemed to be pretty soundproof. While we were inside shooting away at imaginary targets, one or two people were always outside watching for anything suspicious while pretending to do some work in the garden.

After a couple of sessions it was no longer necessary for me to do all the training as group members could now train the other members of the group. In fact, a few months later more agents were dropped for the specific purpose of training the underground forces in Holland. After the war I learned to my surprise that one of those agents was Ludo de Stoppelaar, my friend in Stockholm. He was flown to England two months after I left and had also joined the Special Forces. He had been dropped some time in September so we were operating in the same area for a couple of months.

Transmitter

Chapter Ten

Sinking Ships and Blowing up Trains

Following those first airdrops of supplies I attended a meeting of the leaders of the resistance groups in Rotterdam. One man had heard that the Germans were planning to tow several ships from the Rotterdam harbour to the New Waterway, the only entrance to Rotterdam from the ocean. They planned to load the ships down with cement and rocks and sink them in the Waterway. The tidal movement of the water would make them sink deeper into the silt to the point that it would be very difficult to lift them after the war. This was of great concern since it would mean that Rotterdam would be cut off from the ocean for larger vessels until the ships were removed. Only smaller vessels with a shallow draft would be able to clear the obstructions. Everyone was looking to me for a plan of action, and I said that before we did anything I would like to explain this situation to London and ask them for permission to sink these ships where they were at berth. When London gave us permission, and assuming they had no other plans, I would immediately order some limpets that were explosive devices specifically made for this purpose. Each limpet has six magnets, three on each side, which can be attached to the hull of a ship. That evening I sent a telegram describing the situation and asking permission to sink the ships at berth. The answer came: 'Agree to sink the ships at berth. How many limpets are required'? I immediately ordered six limpets and called on one of the resistance leaders to arrange another meeting with all the leaders. At this meeting one of the leaders suggested that it would be much easier to just open the valves and sink the ships rather than waiting for the limpets. As the ships were not guarded it would be very easy to slip on board and do this and by morning they would be on bottom. I agreed that it would be easier but suggested that it would also be very easy for the Germans to refloat them. All they would have to do was to send a diver down, shut the valves and then pump out the water; in no time the ship would be at the surface again. I also pointed out that from that moment the ships would be heavily guarded and a lot more difficult to get close to them. Most of the leaders agreed with me and decided that it would be preferable to wait for the limpets so that a more permanent job could be done.

So much to my surprise and displeasure, about a week later, there was an announcement by the German commandant in the Rotterdam newspaper that saboteurs had sunk one of the ships in the harbour. He warned that such acts of sabotage would not be tolerated and that if it happened again it would result in severe penalties. I was furious and immediately called one of the leaders and told him that I wanted an explanation for what had happened. Since we had clearly agreed on waiting for the limpets I would have thought that he had enough control over his men that he would not have allowed them to go ahead and sink the ship against our group decision. I added that he must realize it will now be a lot more difficult to get close to any of the ships.

He had little to say in response to my anger and told me later that it had been the work of a group of free-lance saboteurs. I had to come to the conclusion that in this type of business it was absolutely impossible to keep control of everything. After all, we were dealing with a bunch of free spirits who were all out to do as much damage to the enemy as possible without waiting for permission from somebody. I also realized that without such individuals we would not be able to achieve what we all wanted and that was to defeat the Germans in any way we could. However, the result as I had predicted, was that within three days the ship was afloat again; the divers had simply been sent down to close the valves and the water was pumped out.

The limpets arrived and when we surveyed the area where the ships were moored we found out that there now were sentries on board as well as on the wharf. The only way to get close to a ship was to swim with a limpet or try to get a rowboat close to the ship or a combination of a rowboat part of the way and then swim the rest. We tested the waters first, sending a couple of men in a small rowboat on the opposite side of the water pretending that they were fishing. They would slowly move closer to the ship and purposely light a cigarette so that a sentry would be able to detect them. On each occasion they were spotted and had a bright searchlight on them and observed for a while. Then the light was turned off, the observers apparently satisfied that they were dealing with a couple of innocent fisherman. The boatmen could tell by the sound of their boots on the steel deck that the guards were moving away from the railing. The 'fishing trip' was repeated a few more times until we were satisfied that sticking a few limpets to the hull of the ships would be a feasible operation.

On the night of the operation there was a half moon, and we timed it so that the ship was in between the moon and the 'fishermen'. Three limpets were readied with the plan to attach at least two and possibly a third as close as possible to the engine room. The timing device consisted of a firing pin attached to a spring held in closed position by a steel wire that went through a tiny hole to a chamber where it was secured. If anything broke the wire, the spring was released and the firing pin would detonate the charge. A box with six glass vials containing acid of different strengths and were marked one hour, two hours, etc. came with each limpet. The strength of the acid was designed to eat through the wire in the time indicated on the box. We decided to use the four-hour vials in order to give us plenty of time to go to the spot where the 'fishermen' had launched the boat. We would do some 'fishing' to make sure everything was normal, row to the ship, plant the limpets and get away. The tense part of this was that everything had to be prepared before the limpets were taken to the rowboat. The vials had to be inserted into the chamber that held the wire; the chamber was then closed by a screw that crushed the glass releasing the acid to start eating away at the wire.

In Scotland, during the training, we were only shown these devices and told how they worked, but we had never gone through the operation of setting the trigger. Now, when actually doing it with real acid, that was supposed to eat through a wire in a preset time, I realized that there was a lot of room for errors! The strength of the acid could be wrong or the wire could brake prematurely. These were questions going through all our minds and I suppose in particular the minds of the two men that were going to take the limpets to the ship. However, I must make it very clear that during the war, I never once detected any sense of fear in any of the people participating in the resistance. We, and I include myself, did whatever was necessary at the time without any thought of danger.

The operation was completely successful. All three limpets were attached to the targeted ship, and four hours later, long after the two men had returned, all three bombs went off within ten minutes of each other. Everything had gone very smoothly, although I learned afterwards that they did not do much 'fishing' with the time clocks ticking away, and had just kept moving towards the ship to attach the limpets.

Weapon drops were now almost a routine daily occurrence, except for the nights when it was totally dark. Load after load of weapons came into Rotterdam, seemingly without the enemy getting wind of it.

I met one of the men who had been present during the drop that I participated in and he told me that the same site had been used a few more times. The last time it was used the moon was very bright and after the plane dropped its load, they heard loud screams from the village nearby. They saw people on top of the roofs against the light sky and they were all yelling: 'The Allies are coming! The Allies are coming!' It was decided that after such publicity the site would no longer be safe, and it was not used again!

About the middle of September of that year, 1944, 'Operation Market Garden' took place. Thousands of Allied troops and equipment were parachuted into an area a few kilometres north of Eindhoven to the north of the Rhine at Arnhem. The mission was to try to secure the bridges across the Rhine. Unfortunately due to foggy conditions the operation had not gone as planned. There was heavy fighting for days afterwards and it appeared that the Germans were getting the upper hand.

Shortly following 'Operation Market Garden' we received orders from London to blow up as many rail lines as possible north and east of Arnhem to try to prevent German reinforcements getting to the combat area of Arnhem and south of the Rhine where heavy fighting was still taking place. We were to advise London when we were ready to act and then wait for a signal to blow all the lines on the same night to create as much chaos as possible. The signal was to be: 'The geese are flying south' broadcast by the BBC at the regular times of eight and ten in the evening. This was an order close to my heart and I spent the following days instructing members of the resistance on how to apply explosives to a railway so that they were able to go to different parts of the country, taking all the necessary explosives and gadgets with them, to teach other groups. This would maximize the effect of the chaos caused by one single night's mission.

Blowing up a rail line required attaching a detonator with primer cord to two gobs of plastic explosive about six feet behind the detonator and six feet from each other. The detonator was flat and was clamped on top of the rail line with a wire spring; for some strange reason it was called a 'fog signal'. The fog signals were dark grey and barely visible in the dark. The detonator exploded when the wheel of the locomotive went over it and the two explosive charges would blow away the rail line between them causing the locomotive and some of the cars to go off the tracks. We were taught that the best place was just ahead of a bridge because the train would wreck the bridge and part of the train would land in the water;

the faster the train was going the more damage it caused. This project was too tantalizing for me; although it was against my orders I could not resist doing one of the lines myself. I decided on the one coming from Bentheim in Germany, just after it crossed the Dutch border. Fortunately, Bentheim happened to be the stamp on my pass that I was supposed to have received on my way to Holland at the start of my holidays. So if I should run into trouble I could say that I was on my way back to my ship in Hamburg. A few days later I advised London that we were ready to go and boarded the train to the city of Enschede in the north-east of Holland, a few miles from the German border. I dressed in work clothes and with an old navy cap on my head; I looked like an innocent mariner. I brought only a couple of fog signals with me because I knew that there would be plenty of plastic explosive and primer cord available in Enschede.

When I arrived in Enschede I phoned Jeff, one of the leaders of the local underground whom I had met at one of our early meetings, and told him that I had come to see him. We met at a coffee shop close to the station; I explained why I was there and that I needed a bicycle, some explosive, fifteen feet of primer cord, and two men to help me. He gave me the address of a man, Jack, who lived in a small village close to the location where I intended to blow up the rail line and he promised that he would bring me the explosive and the cord the next day. He assured me that Jack would gladly help me and that he would know of somebody else to join us. We went together to a place where he borrowed a bike for me and I was soon on my way to the village. I told Jeff that I would probably not be able to return the bike and asked him if I could leave him a couple of hundred guilders so that he could buy another one, he nodded in agreement accepting the comment without seeming to be overly concerned. Jeff said he would phone Jack to tell him that I was coming and that I would need to stay with him for a few days. The address he had given me was quite easy to find and Jack was expecting me. He introduced me to his wife, showed me the room where I would be staying and asked me when I would like to meet Bill, the other member of our group. I replied as soon as possible since this would mean we would be ready to go whenever we got the signal. He said that they had a radio and listened to the BBC; apparently he had been involved in airdrops, so was used to listening to the BBC news every evening. He seemed to be a very pleasant and capable fellow; he phoned Bill immediately and Bill would come over that night right after dinner.

There was still some time before his wife would have dinner on the table and so we had a few beers and discussed what I was planning to do. He knew a spot where the rail line crossed a bridge and we decided to go there to look over the terrain and to familiarize ourselves with the area. It would be dark when we had finished our job and I was not planning to go back to Jack's place, but to get as far away as possible from the scene of the explosion. I was sure that the Germans would be roaming the countryside as soon as they got word of the explosion, looking for the perpetrators.

Bill arrived soon after we had finished dinner. We chatted for a while and I told him of our plans. He seemed very keen and eager, and I surmised that there had not been much activity the last few months, other than a few airdrops, and that he was ready for some excitement. He pulled a map out of his pocket that showed the whole area in minute detail and said that I could use it for the next few days. We told Bill that we planned to visit the explosion site to assess the situation and suggested that Bill did likewise and we meet again in the afternoon to compare notes.

Early the next morning Jack and I set off on our bicycles; it was a beautiful fall day and I thoroughly enjoyed the countryside. I had not been in this part of Holland before and was surprised at how different it was to the western part of Holland. Despite its proximity to the border there were no German soldiers; it was almost as if there was no occupation. The only evidence of the war had been during the night when we heard the steady drone of Allied bombers overhead on their way to targets in Germany, or going back to England after dropping their bombs. We cycled to where the road crossed the main rail line from Bentheim in Germany. I looked at my map and estimated that we were about four kilometres from the border. We stopped to assess the area and noted where the railroad went across a small bridge; Jack assured me that this would probably be the only bridge for quite a distance. On going a little further we came to a narrow country road that led towards the bridge and there we turned off to get a better look at the bridge and the surrounding terrain. We stopped directly opposite the bridge and estimated that it was about two hundred yards from where we stood. There did not seem to be any houses close by which meant that after the explosion it would be quite a while before anybody would be aware of what had happened. The next station was about three kilometres away and they would probably not be overly concerned if the train was behind time. This would give us plenty of time to get away from the scene so we decided that this was a perfect location to blow up the line. Jack and I spent the rest of the morning traveling all the country roads, in particular the roads leading away from the bridge. By the end of the morning I had a pretty good picture of the area in my mind. We stopped at a small country café to eat and then went home.

There was a message waiting for Jack to call Jeff, who was able to report that he had the explosive and the primer cord and would deliver them that afternoon. I decided to take the opportunity to have a snooze as I had not slept much in the last three or four days and felt tired. When I awoke, Jeff had already come and gone. Then Bill dropped by and we told him where the job was to take place. He too was to listen to the BBC and when he heard the signal message, come to Jack's house so that we could leave together. However, that night the message did not arrive and we went to bed early.

The next day we decided to go out again and check over the whole plan in detail. When we got to the spot opposite the bridge we walked over just to make sure that there were no obstacles when we went there in the dark to install the necessary explosives. As everything seemed to be straight-forward we cycled back to Jack's place. It was not till two days later that the message came through on the eight o'clock broadcast and within a few minutes Bill joined us. We went over the whole plan once more and then Bill left with the explosives. Jack and I left a few minutes later with the primer cord, the fog signal, some tape and a pair of crimping pliers. It was beautiful out, fairly warm and the quarter moon low in the sky gave us just enough light to see around us. When we came to the spot on the narrow road opposite the bridge, Bill was there waiting for us. There was a ditch on either side of the road where we could lay our bicycles down. We walked over towards the bridge and soon we were ready; I had done this so often now that I could do everything almost blind-fold.

On our way back to the road, I suggested that Bill and Jack go back home and that I would leave a few minutes later heading the other way in a westerly direction. I sat on the side of the road while the two disappeared into the night and lit a cigarette. I had originally planned to leave right away, but now decided to go to a spot further down the road where I would still be able to see the train and the explosion. In the stillness of the night I thought that I could hear the faint rumble of a train in the distance, so I got onto my bike and went a few hundred yards down the road to where it went over a small rise. At this spot I decided that this was as good a place as any to watch the oncoming train and the explosion. The sound was louder and almost certainly it was the sound of an approaching train. And 'yes', a few minutes later I could see the train. It appeared to be two passenger cars followed by several flatcars loaded with army equipment of some sort; there could have been tanks or armoured cars, or both, on the flatcars. Then as the engine triggered the detonator the explosion came, followed by the noise of the engine hitting the bridge. The two passenger cars went over on their sides and the flatcars piled in to whatever was ahead of them. I could see steam coming from the engine that seemed to be half submerged in the stream. Everything had gone according to plan.

When I heard voices yelling and moaning I decided that it was high time to leave. I jumped on my bike and headed further west. The noises grew fainter till I could hear nothing. It was about two o'clock in the morning and I still had not met anybody on the road or detected any activity anywhere around me. I planned to be as far as possible from the train wreck before traffic started to flow again. Fortunately I was able to stay on narrow country roads without having to go through towns or cross major high ways.

By six o'clock in the morning I was about sixty kilometres from the scene of the train wreck and figured that nobody could ever suspect me of having had anything to do with the explosion. I came to an intersection on my road signed: 'Zutphen 2 km' and decided that this was as good a place as any to try to board the train to Rotterdam. At the station I found out that there were no trains leaving Zutphen in any direction; passengers for Rotterdam were advised to proceed to Apeldoorn, which is about another twenty kilometres further west. I smiled to hear this because I knew that it was the result of blowing up the rail lines. Later, I learned that similar explosions had occurred in sixteen different places.

The German soldiers were shouting and urging everyone to leave the station. Ignoring them, I went into the restaurant across from the ticket booths; I sat there eating breakfast facing the main entrance hall so that I could watch and enjoy the chaos. The coffee tasted as if it had been made several days ago and reheated umpteen times. The breakfast was not good either but I could not expect much better at that stage of the war. A common expression used in those days was: 'I don't care how it tastes as long as there is lots of it!' When one is hungry, quantity is more important than quality! After breakfast I left, jumped on my bike, and peddled to Apeldoorn. I knew the phone number of one of the local leaders of the underground and gave him a call. I asked him if he could keep the bicycle I had borrowed so that the owner could pick it up later. 'No problem', he said and gave me the directions to a place a few blocks from his house, where he would meet me. When I told him why I had borrowed the bike, he grinned and told me that three of his men had blown up the train further north. They had called him right after the explosion and were now on their way back to Apeldoorn.

I had no problem getting a train for Rotterdam from Apeldoorn and arrived there in the afternoon. When I got home there was a message for me from Didi; she had several wire messages for me and she would bring them over right away. She arrived and we went to my room where we worked on decoding the messages. The first one read: 'Great job stop rail traffic seems in chaos.' The other more routine messages were mainly pertaining to ships they would like to have sunk and asking for details about their locations. I was rather surprised because I thought that they should have been able to get this information from an aerial photograph of the harbour. While in London, I had looked at aerial photographs taken from a height of ten thousand feet and was able to read the engraving on the tombstones in a cemetery! Later, I found out that not only had the Germans done a superb job at camouflaging the ships, but the weather had been so murky that they had been unable to take any pictures. Also, it was now practically impossible to get anywhere near the ships after we sank the one ship about a month ago.

It was now the end of October. The news of the war was becoming increasingly optimistic and it seemed that the Germans were in retreat on all fronts. The Russians were still engaging German troops who had been in retreat ever since the battle of Stalingrad. At the same time it seemed to me that, after the failure of operation Market Garden, the liberation of Holland now had a low priority in favour of pushing east, leaving Holland to be resolved at a later date. I was beginning to have doubts as to whether we would ever be called to rise up in arms and help our Allies to drive the Germans out of Holland. However, airdrops were continuing to take place in every part of Holland.

Chapter Eleven

Arrested and Transported to Germany: 1944

It was the beginning of November, 1944. The war was raging on but it seemed that the Germans would eventually capitulate. This was the opinion of everyone, except of course the Germans. The American first and ninth armies had captured Aachen, the first major city in Germany. The Allies were now almost in control of all the German territory west of the Rhine.

On the first of November the British fifty-second division with three commando groups landed on the garrisoned island of Walcheren in the extreme south-west of Holland. Bad weather denied them sufficient air support but the battleship 'Warspite' and a few other ships provided the gunfire. This operation raised renewed hope that the Allies were going to land on the coast of Holland, drive the German forces out, and liberate Holland. We were poised and ready to rise up behind the lines if and when the order was issued. They were false hopes as no orders came and the news about an invasion soon petered out.

However, something else was brewing on the home front. We kept getting rumours about 'razzias', involving plundering, destructive incursions or raids taking place in other parts of Holland by the German troops. These acts were done in a rude, arrogant, abusive way with complete disregard of human dignity. German troops would completely seal off a large part of a city overnight, and at daybreak they would be everywhere and systematically go from house to house looking for men. Men were taken out of the house and herded into a large open field surrounded by barbed wire and guarded by soldiers every ten or fifteen feet. At night they would be loaded into cattle cars and moved east towards Germany.

On hearing of these 'razzias', I decided immediately to move to a different address so that the safety of the family I was with would not be compromised. I picked a flat on the ground floor that had a separate entrance, and I told Didi to make her deliveries to that address from now on. Just in case I was arrested, I taught Jannie how to code and decode the messages and gave her the last ten pages of the five letter code groups so that she could continue sending messages to London. Finally, I sent a wire to London advising them of my actions and to assure them that Jannie was totally reliable and capable of sending messages on my behalf. She was not going to take a leading role but would solely act as a go-between for the various resistance groups and London. Everyone involved in our groups was familiar with the information required for newly selected drop sites.

The next few days passed uneventfully, but then, on the morning of the eleventh, when I peaked out of my window, I saw German soldiers everywhere. I immediately phoned Jannie and asked her to let London know of what might happen if my identification papers and the letter from the captain of my ship saying that I was to return shortly to Hamburg did not get me off the hook.

In fact the soldiers did not even want to look at any papers. When I asked to speak to the commanding officer they totally ignored me and told me to get out of the house immediately. Outside there were several men in the centre of the road, with scores of German soldiers lined on both sides of the road, many of the soldiers with their fingers on the triggers of their machine pistols. Several hours later we were herded into a rail yard in between two rows of soldiers. Escaping seemed impossible but I heard later that Josh, who had also been arrested, had managed to do so. The rail yard had a high wire fence on both sides and German soldiers guarded the open ends. At first, loudspeakers in all four corners were constantly barking instructions not to try to escape, and any who tried to would be shot. The intervals between the announcements gradually became a little longer, and in the early afternoon it was announced that we would be supplied with food. This was good news since I was beginning to feel very hungry, though I did not expect much. Finally potato and cabbage soup was dished out in metal bowls with a small hunk of bread. When a person is hungry, quality becomes the least of one's concerns.

As night approached it got chilly and dark and we were all wondering what was going to happen next. Suddenly the yard lights came on and a few minutes later several huge floodlights came on which were mounted on army trucks outside the fence and at both ends of the yard. Throughout the day, women and children had gathered outside the fences trying to find their loved ones inside the fence. The German soldiers were constantly shouting at them to stay away from the fence. The women and children would back away but they would soon return and after a while they just ignored the soldiers and stayed where they were.

About midnight a long train of boxcars slowly backed into the yard; the doors of the boxcars opened;

a step was placed at each of the doors of the first four cars and the men were ordered inside. I was on the other side of the cars, so I could not see what was happening, but from the shouts of the soldiers it wasn't difficult to guess that people were being herded into the cars. When the first four cars were loaded, they shut the doors and the train moved forward until the next four empty cars were in place. And so it went on until all the people on that side of the train were inside the boxcars. The train then slowly moved till the last boxcar was outside the enclosure. The guards then ordered us all to move to the other side; it was not difficult to guess what was going to happen to the rest of us.

At that moment I heard somebody on the other side of the fence calling my name. I waited. Then again I heard my name. This time I was sure that someone was calling me. I started moving towards the fence in the direction of the voice as I thought that I recognized Jannie's voice. Yes, there she was just on the other side of the fence. She motioned for me to come closer and told me that she had not heard back from London; also that Josh had managed to escape. That was good news. I told her that I would try to escape but the Germans seemed to be very trigger-happy so I would wait for an opportunity later. Just then a soldier nearby ordered us to move away from the fence. I shouted to her not to worry about me, to carry on the good work and to say hello to everybody. When I looked back, she had disappeared into the crowd.

When all the men were on the other side of the tracks, the train moved back and the rest of the boxcars were filled with their human cargo. It was a very humiliating experience that made me very angry. We were so cramped that only some could sit down on the floor while the rest had to remain standing. There were no toilet facilities and we were wondered if they would make any stops to let us out to relieve ourselves. The doors were shut and it was pitch black inside except for the light coming in through two high small barred windows and holes or cracks in the wall. I looked at my watch and could just make out that it was just after midnight.

Finally, at around three o'clock the train started moving very slowly but after a while it stopped again. We could see through the cracks that we were at the Central Station of Rotterdam. There were lots of soldiers on both sides and we could hear commands being shouted by the officers. After a while there was silence and the train moved slowly out of the station and gradually picked up speed. We were all very tired and somehow, in the dark, gradually 'wiggled' ourselves into comfortable positions. I was soon soundly asleep, only vaguely aware that the train was making a few stops. When I woke I realized that I really needed to relieve myself, and that there was no toilet in the car. I could smell the odour of urine and the fact that some men had just urinated on the floor. I yelled: 'Let's not piss all over the place, pretty soon the smell will be unbearable. We should designate a couple of spots in the back of the car.' There was a general mumble of agreement just as the train came to a halt. The doors were opened and we heard shouts of 'Eraus, Eraus!' (Out, Out!). German soldiers had stationed themselves in a row about fifty feet away from the train with their fingers on the triggers of their sub-machine guns. We all jumped out, glad to have the opportunity to relieve ourselves but realized that any attempt to escape would give the guards an excuse to gun you down, and certain death.

Where the train had stopped the countryside somehow looked different; we could see a few farmhouses in the distance and soon realized that we were now in Germany. After a night in the boxcar, the fresh air smelled nice and it certainly felt good to be able to stretch our limbs and walk around a bit. A few men from our car went to see one of the soldiers and I overheard them asking to see the commanding officer. I surmised that they were members of the pro-Nazi, Dutch Socialist Party, and were trying to negotiate their release. When the soldier just motioned them away, they showed him their membership cards, but he just ignored them. It gave me a lot of pleasure to see this and also I knew that I would have to be to be careful what I said if any of these people were close to me.

After a while, just as we were all wondering if they would ever give us something to eat, they came with buckets of hot "ersatz" (artificial) coffee and boxes with hunks of bread, one of each for each car. They also brought a limited number of tin cups, so we had to try to gulp the coffee down while it was still hot so that each man got a turn. Sopping the cold bread in the coffee helped the coffee cool off faster. The coffee really hit the spot despite the fact that it tasted terrible, far worse than the artificial coffee we had at home. Twenty minutes later it was all finished and we were ordered back into the boxcars.

The atmosphere in the boxcars improved considerably once we had something in our stomachs. Somebody noticed a hole in the wooden floor and asked if anybody had a penknife to try to make it larger so that we could use it to pee through. There were several men with penknives, and then others found holes in the floor that could also be enlarged for the same purpose. People started to talk to each other and the fact that the Germans had not paid any attention to the sympathizers had been noticed. Soon the Nazi sympathizers were being scoffed and sneered at and were at the receiving end of derogatory remarks; at one point they were pretty close to being mobbed. Even though they had received the same treatment by the Germans as everybody else, people still felt that they were responsible. The fact that they kept completely silent saved them from a worse fate.

Chapter Twelve

Living and Working in Germany, Sabotage: 1944-1945

Towards evening the train pulled into a station, the doors of our car were opened, and we were ordered to get out and assemble on the platform. A second car was opened and the people ordered out to join us. Then the doors closed again and the train departed. Had we arrived at our final destination, Bamberg? There were, about a hundred of us, on the platform of the station, guarded by about a dozen German soldiers. They marched us out of the station to a large barrack where we stayed for the next few days. The barrack room had four rows of cots, four rows of long tables with benches on each side, a small kitchen area with a stove and a sink, and a couple of washrooms and toilets. The Germans would bring in a big pot of soup, potatoes, and cabbage and we were dished up a spoonful of each. The soup was cabbage soup; cabbages must have been in plentiful supply as this was the only vegetable we ate for a few weeks. Finally, we got to know our way around and discovered that there were other vegetables available.

Another discovery was that there was a rendering plant in Bamberg where one could pick up bones for free. These we would boil for days and were surprised at how much fat we could still get from them; enough to fry up some potatoes and the odd piece of meat that we managed to get. Bamberg was a small, very old, quaint city about fifty kilometres north of Nurnberg. The day following our arrival, we had a visit from some German officials who told us where we were going to be put to work. A few jobs were available with the German railroad and I immediately applied for that work. I showed them my papers, and told them that I was actually on holidays when I was picked up in Rotterdam, and that I was supposed to report back for work in Hamburg; also that if I ever ran into an ID check, I would be found AWOL (absent without leave) and be in real trouble. Even if I went back now I would be late and still be in serious trouble. The official seemed to understand my predicament and suggested that I stay in Bamberg and work for the railroad. He explained that they had a serious personnel trouble and that he thought that I would be of use in Bamberg and suggested that the shipping company would never find out my whereabouts.

I said that was just fine but that I would need to have legitimate papers complete with a valid ID, indicating that I was working here for the 'Deutsche Reichsbahn'. This is how I managed to get a new identity as 'Herr Dykerman' with a complete set of 'legitimate' papers under yet another false name! I was given the job of 'packmeister' and supplied with a uniform, a duffel coat, a pair of felt boots, and a cap; I could hardly believe my luck. Here I found myself, an operative of the Allies, in the heart of enemy territory with papers in my pocket issued by the enemy! As a 'packmeister', I had to ride with the mail cars and sort out the mail, mostly parcels but some letters while we were traveling.

Later I discovered that all foreign workers were restricted to an area within one kilometre of their place of work, but there were no such restrictions imposed on me. Two more men from the group were also

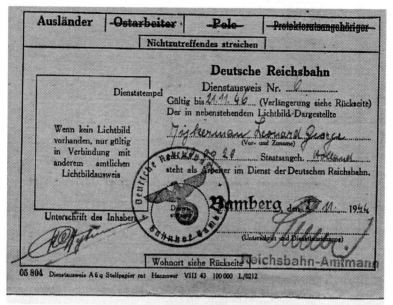

Official ID issued by the 'Deutsche Reichsbahn' in my false name

chosen to work as 'packmeisters' and I often ended up working in the same baggage car with one of them. One was a school teacher, and the other, an office manager. All three of us could ride the trains for free. The baggage cars contained all sorts of parcels and boxes and I spent the first few weeks looking at who were the senders and the recipients. Several items were addressed to army units at the front, some items marked 'Secret', and some marked 'Rush', some with both. Other items looked liked parcels being sent to soldiers at the front by their parents and loved ones at home.

I came to the conclusion that there were lots of opportunities for sabotage. During those first few weeks I found out that the other two Dutch men working in the car with me were also fiercely anti-Nazi and were quite willing to help me. I suggested that we should commit sabotage as much as possible while on the job. They were both very willing but admitted they would not have a clue what to do and how to do it. This was not a problem; I would teach them all they needed to know.

Once that was agreed, any time we were alone on the platform, I would show them the oil cups for the wheel axles and how to make them inoperable simply by throwing a handful of fine sand in them which would eventually block the oil line. Axles without oil would soon overheat, seize up or cause a fire, preferably both. In Scotland I had been taught how to set a steam locomotive in motion. At the time it seemed of little importance and I paid little attention to the instructions; I did not think I would ever need to know how to do this. But here now, I had the perfect opportunity! If we were in a train station when the air raid sirens sounded, everybody was ordered to go to a shelter about a hundred yards away from the station. My Dutch friend and I managed to stay together but we did not know where the rest of the train crew was. I decided on one occasion to slip out of the shelter before the all-clear and walk back to the train, just to check if anybody had stayed behind as a safety precaution. I was surprised to find the station and the train totally deserted. I made some loud noises and called the engineer of the locomotive, but there was no answer. So, I went back to my baggage car, curled up in a corner and fell asleep.

I must have slept right through the all-clear siren as I woke up to the sound of the voices of the other personnel in the car and the passengers on the platform returning to the train. I got up from my corner and joined the others. Nobody had noticed that I had been in the car rather than having just returned from the air raid shelter. I realised that if this ever happened again, I could safely stay behind and perhaps set the train in motion without detection.

I told nobody of my plans, deciding I could do this alone and did not need any help, but it was to be quite a while before an opportunity presented itself again. However, in the meantime I familiarized myself with the workings of a steam locomotive, very carefully and as casually as possible to avoid rousing suspicion. I wished that I had paid more attention in Scotland!

As the war progressed it became more and more obvious that the Allies were not going to quickly liberate the western part of Holland, but almost daily the BBC news reported heavy fighting in eastern Holland along the German border. This news made me realize that it was easier for me to inflict damage on the enemy located where I was than it would have been if I had still been in Holland. In my present situation it was much easier for me to move around, and I no longer had to avoid ID checks. After all, the Germans considered me as an ally and had no reason to be suspicious.

My Dutch friend, Erik, and I would often go for a beer in the evening, usually to a small pub that seemed to be popular with the German officers. One evening, as we came in to the dimly lit entrance hall, I noticed a couple of officers take off their belts with the pistol holder, buckle the belt, and hang it on the coat hooks by the entrance. They went into the pub and I took the opportunity to check the holders. I was amazed to find that the pistols were still in them and that officers would leave their weapons unattended in such a public place.

I hung my coat on the same hook over the belts and we went inside. During the evening, other officers arrived and we noticed not all of them gave the 'Heil Hitler' salute upon entering. They were all older soldiers and most seemed to know one another. When we left about an hour later retrieving our coats from the hook, the belt with the pistol was still there. As we walked home an idea began to form in my mind and as soon as I was home and alone I tried an experiment. I took my belt off, buckled it up, and hung it on a coat hook. Then I hung my coat over top of it just as I had done at the pub, grabbed my coat and the belt at the same time, stuck my right arm through the belt and into my coat sleeve, and finished putting my coat on without buttoning it up. When I looked at myself in the mirror I couldn't see that there was a belt underneath my coat. I took my coat off again, tied a shoe onto the belt where the pistol holder would normally be, and repeated the experiment. As long as I let my coat hang loose there was absolutely no evidence that there was something underneath it and certainly nobody would notice anything in the dark or even in dim light. I was pleased and determined to do the same with an officer's belt and pistol next time I had the opportunity at the pub. In the following weeks, I managed to perform this trick several times; on the way home I would throw the pistol in the canal and the belt into a garbage can. It surprised me at first that the officers continued to leave their belts with their pistols in the entranceway. Then it dawned on me that none of them had mentioned the disappearance of their belt and pistol to any of the other officers or to their superiors for fear of punishment!

In time I got to know several Germans who were fiercely anti-Hitler and who readily expressed their feelings in the company of foreigners. Of course they knew that we were not there by choice. One German told me that he had a radio at home and that I was welcome to come over if I wanted to listen to the BBC news. The conversation went roughly as follows:

'Oh, thank you! I will certainly take you up on your offer.'

'I live in an apartment and when you come, just give one knock on the door and I will let you in. Please come fairly late at night because I don't know if all the others in the building can be trusted.'

'By the way, I know an old lady whose son is in the army and is very anti-Hitler. If you are looking for a place to stay, I am sure that she will rent you a room.'

'Yes, I would like very much to do that!'

He gave me the old lady's address and I went straight over there. I had had enough of the barracks where we were staying and I was earning enough to pay the rent.

'Frau Müller', who was in her seventies, turned out to be a jewel; she immediately made me feel at home. When I told her how I had come to be in Bamberg, she knew that she could trust me and let me listen to the BBC on her radio at any time. She told me that her son, Carl, had a PhD in chemistry, had never joined any of the Nazi organizations, and had never got above the rank of corporal. If he had been pro-Nazi, with his education, he would at least have the rank of colonel. When I came home in the evening, she would offer me a cup of tea, a bowl of soup, or a sandwich. She treated me like her own son and, although I never told her my real background, she seemed to intuitively sense that I was not just a forced labourer. At Christmas Frau Müller invited me for dinner, along with a few of her German friends. They were also elderly people and quite pleasant company. No one talked about the war all evening, and the roast chicken dinner was delicious.

At first, the German chief of our baggage car kept a close watch on us and taught us how to sort the parcels, which compartment to put them in depending on their destination. We were told to be very particular with any box with an army address on it, because those could be important spare parts headed for the front in the west. They were easy to identify, since the more important they were, the more stickers they had: URGENT, FIRST PRIORITY, WITH CARE, sometimes TOP SECRET, etcetera. As long as he kept a close watch on us we were very careful to do things right, but after a while, when he felt that he could leave us alone, he usually curled up in a corner and went to sleep. This was our chance! From then on, we took every opportunity to put parcels into the wrong compartment, especially the more important ones. The parcels marked: 'with care' would, of course, be treated extra rough; dropping them on the floor while keeping an eye on the chief; if he didn't look up we would pick them up again and really smashed them! In addition to the military parcels, we handled parcels to individual soldiers who were at the front lines. Sometimes we would poke a hole in them, take things out, usually edible items, and replace them with garbage. As I write this today, almost fifty years later, I can hardly believe that I did these things. What terrible things to do, but at that time and in those circumstances they seemed the 'right thing to do'. Our minds were in 'war mode' and everything we did to disrupt the war effort of the enemy, or to hurt the moral of the men was fair game.

As the Allied troops advanced further east, it became increasingly dangerous for the trains to travel by day. Allied fighter planes were in the sky all day long with very little resistance from the German fighters. Trains seemed to be their main target; they were attacked by approaching from behind, with guns firing with the objective of shooting holes into the locomotive boilers. One hole was enough to destroy a boiler since being under pressure it would blow itself empty and collapse. So most of our trips were now made during the hours of darkness; the Germans could ill afford the loss of locomotives that were their main means of transportation.

One night while traveling south towards Nürnberg, the train stopped in the middle of nowhere and we were all ordered to get out and move as far away from the train as possible. As we left the train we could see that the sky to the south of us was brightly lit and at the same time we could hear the drone of heavy bombers heading in the direction of the lit up sky. Wave after wave of bombers came over us all heading in the same direction and dropping their load of bombs inside the area that had been marked by the scout planes. The bombardment lasted almost four hours and when everything was quiet again we were told to get back on the train which proceeded towards Nürnberg. When we reached the outskirts of the city, the train stopped and we assumed that the engineer was waiting for daylight before proceeding further into the heart of the city. Fires burning near the city centre were clearly visible and we could smell the stench of the smoke. As daylight came we slowly headed towards the city, but a few minutes later the train stopped again. We could go no further as the rail yard was totally destroyed. The marshalling yards had been the main target of last night's bombing and hardly a rail remained horizontal. Most of the passengers gathered their belongings and started walking towards the centre of the city but we received orders to go back to the previous station, to unload all the baggage, and to wait till after dark before going back to Bamberg.

Almost every night we heard the heavy bombers on their way to some target to the east or north of us. Sometimes the air raid sirens went off and we all were supposed to go into a shelter, but I never did like to go into those shelters; they were hot and humid and, with everybody smoking, the air soon became unbearable. One day I decided to go outside the town to a hayfield and stay out in the open during the air raid. I took a pillow and lay down fully clothed with my felt boots, my duffel overcoat, my cap, and a warm scarf around my neck, my hands tucked inside my coat. I was warm as toast and soon fell asleep; from then on I never went inside a shelter. Often, I missed hearing the all-clear signal and would wake up hours later, even though the temperature was seldom above zero. When I came home to Bamberg Frau Müller was always there, ready to make me breakfast.

One night in late January 1945, our train was on its way west towards Frankfurt and while we were stopped at a small station the siren went off. Everybody immediately left for the shelters; that is, everybody except me. I stayed inside the car until everyone else had gone. The platform appeared to be totally abandoned. This was the chance to do something that I had been planning for several weeks. I walked casually towards the engine and called: 'Is anybody there?' No answer! Overhead the heavy bombers kept up a steady drone that would drown out any noise that I might make. I climbed up the steps and found myself at the controls of the steam engine. It was pitch black. I checked the platform again to make sure no one was around and then opened the fire door a bit to give me some light. The coals immediately came to life and I knew that I could not leave the door open long before the pressure relief valve would open. I found the brake handle and released the brakes. Immediately the train started to move and as it did so I quickly closed the door and jumped out; my heart was pounding from excitement. I had done it! In my imagination I saw the train barrelling down the track and coming to an abrupt stop somewhere in the distance. The train was picking up speed and by the time the last car cleared the station it was going at a pretty good clip.

About half an hour later the all clear sounded and the personnel and passengers started coming back to the station. I mingled with them trying to spot the engineer and other members of the crew. When I heard the engineer swearing and cursing, I started walking towards him. Other crewmembers started yelling at the engineer, accusing him for what had happened. I joined in the chorus and was relieved that nobody had noticed that I had not been in the shelter. The darkness had helped; but the fact that the tracks sloped down to the west was perhaps the reason why they never suspected foul play and concluded that it was the result of an accidental chain of events. I never found out where and how the train had ended up. Who knows? Perhaps a night fighter had spotted the train and blown up the engine or maybe it had run into another train. I hoped so! Unfortunately that was my only opportunity for such an act and perhaps it was just as well because orders were issued that at least one person had to stay behind to guard the train, and the engineers were told that they were to apply the emergency brake before they left the engine.

Since the beginning of December the BBC news had not been so good while the German news was very upbeat. The Germans had apparently started a major counter-offensive to try to retake all of Belgium including the port of Antwerp. The Allies were hampered by bad weather and unable to supply sufficient air support. We had become used to good news every day, so this put quite a damper on me. When the weather cleared the Allies were at last able to launch a major counter-offensive and drive the Germans back to where they had started. By the end of January, the battle, known as the Battle of the Bulge, was declared officially over. I breathed easier again!

The 'redirection' of mail and parcels had by this time become almost a routine activity. My two Dutch friends and I managed to disrupt the regular flow of mail and parcels by making the address illegible, or by putting them in the wrong slot, or both.

Just outside Bamberg was the second biggest ammunition factory in Germany. We did not realise this until one day, there were very heavy explosions causing the windows to shake and rattle. As it was during the day, we decided to walk in the direction of the explosions. We could see nothing but a few small columns of smoke in the distance and decided to go a little closer. Suddenly there was a huge explosion followed by a blast of air, so strong that it literally knocked us back on our seats six feet from where we had been standing. We saw another column of smoke almost in direct line with the others and decided to stay where we were to see what happened next. There was a small hill nearby and we sheltered behind it in case there was another explosion. Half an hour later there was another explosion and within seconds once more a strong flow of air going over us. During the next three hours we remained behind the hill and every twenty or thirty minutes, there was another explosion. Judging by the columns of smoke the explosions seemed to be getting closer all the time. Strangely we became used to the explosions and quite bored with the whole thing, but it was a warm and sunny day and as there was no reason to be in town we decided to stay and simply enjoy the sunshine. As time passed others joined us to watch and told us that it was a huge underground ammunitions factory that was causing the explosions.

Apparently, what had happened was that a train, just emerging from the factory above the ground was spotted by a few Allied fighters who immediately attacked the engine and the few cars behind it. The engine was put out of commission and the boxcars loaded with ammunition exploded. This had set off a chain reaction, and, since most of the train was still underground, it eventually ignited part of the plant itself. A German who was familiar with the plant explained it was built in sections fifty feet or so apart, each with its own loading facilities. The workers were Ukrainian women; I wondered if they had been able to escape. I had not seen any large facilities to house the thousands of women and he told me that the women worked, ate and slept underground and never came out. An icy chill came over me as I realized that all these women never had a chance and probably perished with the first big explosion. This was another of these horrendous things that, during the course of the war, one just learned to accept without getting too upset. During the German campaign into the USSR thousands of soldiers on both sides and thousands of civilians perished during the Russian winter. There was very little news released from the Russian front by the Germans after the battle of Stalingrad, but we knew from the BBC news broadcasts that the Germans had been beaten back to well into Poland and were offering little resistance.

There were several more explosions during that day at the munitions plant, and then they stopped. When almost an hour had passed since the last explosion we decided to go back to town. I was met by Frau Müller at the top of the stairs who asked me about these big explosions. She said that she had felt the house shake and that her dishes had rattled in the cupboards; then she offered me something to eat, an offer I accepted gratefully as I had not had anything to eat for quite a while and I was really hungry.

We went quite often to a pub located on the outskirts of the town. It was mainly frequented by local farmers and railroad workers and had a very relaxed atmosphere. It was run by the owner, his wife and a young woman who was the waitress. The young woman's husband was at the eastern front and she had not heard from him for months. I found out quite quickly that they were all fiercely anti-Nazi, but as long as there were German customers in the pub, the war was never discussed. They had learned over the years never to trust a fellow German, and even though most of them knew, or sensed, that the war could not possibly last much longer it had not loosened their tongues. But as soon as the German customers left, the owner of the pub felt free to open up and discuss the latest BBC news. The young waitress said little but her occasional remarks left no doubt that she had no use for the Nazis even though her husband was fighting in the army.

There was a Russian POW camp quite close to Bamberg. About twenty or thirty of the POWs were employed at, and around, the railroad station doing general clean-up work. They were all skin and bones and were always guarded by at least one German soldier. We were forbidden to talk to them or give them anything, but we soon found a way to slip them some food now and then that we had pilfered from the parcels. Once in a while when the guard was some distance away I talked to some of them; they knew they could trust us. Some were obviously well educated; I asked one of them what he did before the war he told me that he was a university professor of music. I asked him if he thought the Russians and the west were going to be friends after the war. He looked at me for quite a while before he answered that he did not believe that they would be quite ready for that to happen. I could not understand what he meant. I thought that here we were, both fighting the Germans, with the United States supplying them with thousands of tons of war material, and yet they were not ready to be friends when it was all over. 'Friends at war and enemies in peace.' How right he turned out to be!

One morning after that conversation they found the bodies of about twenty Russian POW's scattered in the rail yard. They had escaped from the camp during the night, had broken the lock on the valve of a tank car loaded with methyl alcohol and had drunk themselves to death. The Germans were furious, not only at the guards on duty during the night but also at the Russians who were treated extra harshly during the next few days. Some who had survived their drinking bout died later.

The mood of the Germans had changed considerably during the last few months. They no longer had that confident, triumphant look, sometimes with a smirk on their faces. They obviously realized that the war was lost and that it was only a matter of time before the inevitable surrender. In the meantime they watched their cities being laid to ruins by the endless Allied bombardments. Almost every night one could hear the heavy drone of bombers on their way to targets further east. They would no longer look you straight in the face but would rather look the other way to avoid seeing the triumphant look on our faces.

During these few months I had met quite a few Germans who were not pro-Hitler, on the contrary they were very anti-Hitler. Some had spent a few years in a concentration camp in the early thirties because they had opposed Hitler. They never changed their minds after they were released and were given menial jobs. They were given a uniform but were never considered part of the regular army and of course were looked down on by the pro-Hitler Germans. I had never realized before that there was such a significant number of Germans who were anti-Hitler. Up till then I had considered all Germans as the enemy. It was quite a revelation and I wondered why the rest of the world had not been aware of this; had they just ignored this fact?

At this time, in February of 1945, all the Allied troops were still west of the Rhine. This situation changed suddenly on March the seventh. The early evening BBC news announced that the Allies had crossed the Rhine at Remagen, a hamlet just south of Bonn. Miraculously the railroad bridge had not been blown up by the Germans and had even survived numerous Allied bombings in the area. Thousands of men and hundreds of tanks of the US First Army poured across the Rhine. Ten days later the bridge collapsed but by then there was a significant unstoppable force on the east side of the Rhine. The bridge was soon repaired and other bridges were built a few days later.

The German army was now in full retreat and as far as I was concerned it was the end of the war for me. I decided to move into the country and told Frau Müller of my intentions and that I was going to stay with the farmer where I had, on occasion, picked up some potatoes and fresh vegetables for her. When I approached the farmer with my scheme, he immediately said that I was welcome to stay in the hayloft and that he would provide me with my meals. I thanked him and went up into the loft where I met three Germans, obviously anti-Nazi, who had also come to stay at the farm a few days earlier.

The next few days were spent in happy anticipation of things to come. I was enjoying the countryside and my days were spent helping the farmer with some chores. It felt so good to be doing something normal, something not connected with the war, but during the still of the night we could hear the guns of the advancing Allied army. Every night they were louder than the night before and then we started to hear them during the day as well.

One day, all of a sudden, we could see jeeps coming around the corner followed by armoured cars and tanks. I ran to the road and reached the road just as the first jeep got there. I waved at them and shouted: 'I am Dutch, glad you are here.' They stopped but the guy next to the driver had his sub-machine gun trained on me and shouted back: 'Deutsch?'
'No, Dutch not Deutsch, Hollander'. He laughed, threw me a pack of cigarettes and they carried on. The Allies were now advancing almost without resistance, at least in the part of Germany where I was but I did hear that the British and Canadians were still meeting stiff resistance in the northwest.

When I went back to the farm I was met by a girl who was crying; she threw her arms around me. She was Jewish and had been in hiding at the farm ever since the persecution of the Jews had begun. It was hard to belief that the farmer had hid her and her mother for all those years without detection. I saw their hiding place, a tiny room underground with a cleverly concealed entrance in one of the kitchen cupboards. They were only able to go outside after dark to get some fresh air. They were living in Bamberg when in 1937 the Germans had arrested the father who ended up in a concentration camp. It was then that they decided to go into hiding and had been living there for almost eight years. That evening the farmer treated us all to a big roast dinner, something we had not had for quite some time. He was even able to produce a few bottles of wine making the evening about as perfect as it could be.

When I woke up the next day, I had a fever and decided to see a doctor. The Americans had a small field hospital not far from the farm and this is where I decided to go. The doctor very quickly diagnosed that I had German measles and I was taken to a larger field hospital further behind the lines where I stayed for the next six days. All the other men in the ward had been wounded and I was the only one that was just 'sick'. After the wake-up call everybody had to turn on his side and expose his behind to receive a penicillin shot. I asked the nurse what kind of a shot she was going to give me; when she told me I protested and told her why I was there. She was good enough to ask a doctor who told her that I should not get a penicillin shot. However, the next morning with a different nurse, it took me a while to convince her that I should not get the shot. Of course to be fair, I was not the first one to protest; there were always patients who tried to avoid a shot. When the doctor came by later that morning, I asked him to write a note that I could pin to my bed to tell the nurses not to give me penicillin. None of the soldiers in the hospital was seriously wounded and there was a happy atmosphere in the ward. Most of them anticipated that this probably meant the end of the war and some were even anticipating going home to the United States. My stay in a field hospital was quite an experience for me. Cigarettes were passed out for free and it was a treat to be smoking good tobacco again after all the horrible substitute tobaccos we had been smoking. I could not get over that new feeling that there was plenty of everything and that everyone else seemed to think that this was quite normal.

When I was released from hospital I hitched a ride back to Bamberg where I reported to the Security

Headquarters. They took me to the office of the commanding officer where I introduced myself and asked them to phone a number in London where there would be someone who would be able to identify me. I was astounded when he became very angry and I heard somebody behind me say: 'Why don't we just shoot the bastard!' Now it was my turn to become angry and I told them that I was not going to answer any questions until they had called the number I had given them. As far as I was concerned they had no reason reacting the way they did. The next three days I was confined, locked up, in a room together with three high ranking Nazis. Somehow they sensed that I was not 'one of them' as they spoke to each other in whispers so that I was unable to hear what was said. This suited me fine because I wanted nothing to do with them. I could not resist once in while drawing my index finger across my throat with a big smile on my face. I can still see the scared look on their faces when I did this. Three days later I was taken to the CO's office where I was introduced to a British officer. He asked me a few questions that only I could have known the answer to and then told the Americans that I was free to go. He said that someone would be sent to pick me up and take me back to London.

The American officers shook hands with me, apologized profusely, and explained to me why they reacted the way they did. Apparently, about a week before I came in, someone had given them an almost identical story. When they phoned London they got an earful and were told that they should not be so gullible and that he was a double agent trying to penetrate the American Intelligence. I had the misfortune of walking in just one week later.....! We all had a good laugh about it whereupon the CO told me that as long as I was in Bamberg I was to be their guest. He instructed one of his underlings to supply me with a jeep, a case of cigarettes, and a half dozen bottles of whiskey. I was totally perplexed at the extreme generosity, but thanked him, shook hands and left. It was quite a sensation to be driving a vehicle myself after all these years and it felt good.

My first visit was to Frau Müller who had no idea where I had been the last few weeks and did not expect to ever see me again. She told me that I was welcome to stay at her house as long as I wanted. I went back to the jeep to fetch the whiskey and the case of cigarettes and took it to my room. Then I asked her to come down to see what I had outside. She was very surprised when she saw the jeep. 'Ach Herr Dykerman, I have always suspected that you were not just a foreign worker!' I smiled at her and acknowledged that I knew that she had probably guessed my identity.

My next visit was to the farmer who had put me up for a few days. Of course, he too was surprised to see me driving a US Army jeep and told me that the Jewish lady and her daughter had moved back into their house in Bamberg. He gave me their address and there was another happy reunion. They invited me to dinner and we had a very pleasant evening. When I asked her if she knew where her husband was, she gave no answer for a long time and just stared into the distance. Then she said that she did not think she would ever see him again.

PART IV

Chapter Thirteen

Germany Surrenders, back to England and getting married: 1945

Germany finally surrendered on May 7, 1945 and soon we heard about and saw pictures of the horrendous concentration camps and the survivors. It was hard to believe that such atrocities could happen, and then to realize that this added even more justification as to why we had fought this war. Many Germans were equally aghast at the sight of the pictures and genuinely horrified, and I had to conclude that Hitler and his cronies had done all the dirty work. I knew now what had probably happened to all those thousands of Jews who had been hauled out of Holland, Belgium and France and that few of them would ever return.

I frequently visited the pub where I spent many pleasant hours. This time when I came in it was almost full. The owner introduced the other patrons to me as his friends and I soon discovered that they all hated the Nazis, but during the war they had said nothing. They had been silent all these years, because they knew all too well that there were people who would report them to the authorities at the drop of a hat. Now, after living so long with this secrecy, it was difficult for them, and also for me, to adjust to the freedom we had now regained; to realize that we could now freely speak our mind. I went back to the jeep to fetch a couple of bottles of whiskey that I had saved for this occasion and presented them to the owner of the pub who in turn poured everybody a glass. When I finally left around midnight the party was still in full swing.

The following morning I heard from the CO of the US Intelligence in Bamberg that there was somebody in his office who was going to take me back to London. I packed my belongings, said goodbye to Frau Müller, thanked her again for taking such good care of me, and hoped that she would have her son back soon. She was in tears and wished me good luck. She was a good old soul!

I threw my stuff in the jeep and drove to the intelligence office where I was met by the same British officer who had come to identify me a few days earlier. He had come with an army vehicle and told me that we were to drive to a place north of Hamburg. 'Preferably a long way from Bamberg', I thought but did not ask questions. I was happy to go anywhere as long as I was on my way to London. It was indeed a long drive and it was dark when we finally arrived at a huge house where I was shown my bedroom and told that I would be flying to London in a few days.

I went to bed right away and woke up early the next day. From my bedroom window I saw a huge lawn sloping down towards a river. Since we were north of Hamburg, I knew that this was the river Elbe. It was strange to recall that not very long ago I had been on the river several times on the way to Sweden or from Sweden to unload our cargo of lumber. My bedroom was very large with an ensuite bathroom with a large tub and a separate shower. When I opened the shower door I saw something I had never seen before; there were four showerheads in each corner and four in the ceiling, and a number of coloured light switches. When I switched on the red one, the whole shower lit up in red. I could have a shower in several different colours! What nonsensical decadence, I thought. I had never before had the experience of being showered by twenty showerheads at the same time! The temperature was controlled by a large chrome wheel. I got dressed and went downstairs into a huge living room that had organ pipes built into the walls just below the ceiling all around the huge living room. The living room led out onto a large deck with a gorgeous view of the river and beyond. I wondered who used had been the owner of this deluxe place and later found out that it was a German general who was married to the daughter of Mr. Messerschmitt, the owner of the aircraft manufacturing plant of the same name. After three days of relaxation in this extraordinary house the same British Officer appeared again. This time he drove me to an airport about sixty miles southwest of Hamburg where I boarded a plane that took me back to England.

My emotions during the plane ride to England were mixed and are hard to describe. After six extraordinary and eventful years of war I could not get used to the fact that it was now all over. At the same time I was enjoying the prospect of seeing some of my friends in London again. My flight arrived late in the afternoon, and I was met by an officer with Special Operation Executive, S.O.E.[7] who drove me to London.

I was stay in a large house there until I had written my report, and until that was completed and I was 'cleared', I was to have no contact with anybody outside. Today, I presume this would be called de-briefing. Naturally, this was a huge disappointment as

---

[7] Special Operations Executive

I had expected to whoop it up with my friends that same night. I was sharing a room with Huib Lauwers who, I later learned, had played a major role in the infamous England Spiel, a highly successful deception scheme of the German Military Intelligence that had come to an end shortly before I was dropped into Holland in 1944.

I decided to waste no time and after dinner sat down at the writing desk and started writing my report. I thought, the sooner I finish this the sooner I am out of here. But Huib, who had been dropped into Holland in 1942 and had been arrested shortly after, not surprisingly wanted to talk. He had been held in solitary confinement for almost two years and had spent the last nine months in a concentration camp in Germany. So we talked till after midnight. He told me all about the England Spiel scheme and how he had tried to warn the Allies who did not seem to get the message. The system devised, to be used by those agents arrested by the Germans, to warn the British Intelligence had not worked. This was a surprise and a shock to me because I had been convinced that in the event I was caught, all I had to do is change the security check and they would know that I was in enemy hands. When we finally decided to call it a night and he was changing into his pyjamas I had a glimpse of his rear end. I had never seen anything like it before: he had no buttocks! His backside looked like skin over bones. When he saw the look on my face, he said: 'That's the way we all were in the concentration camp.'

The next morning I started on my report immediately after breakfast and had finished it before midday. I called the number the SOE officer had given me to tell him that it was ready and, anticipating my release, started packing my bag. As I finished packing the officer arrived, and after checking my report, he signed my release papers. He accompanied me to the officer's supply depot where I was issued with a military uniform. Only then did I realize that I was still in civilian clothes and I became quite anxious to exchange them for a battle dress.

By four o'clock that afternoon I was able to step into the free world complete with new battle dress, new shoes, a red beret and the insignia of a captain of the paratroopers, the rank to which I had been promoted while still behind the lines. I was told that most of my friends were staying at the Cumberland Hotel opposite Hyde Park Corner and they had reserved a room for me there. I had spent many days in this hotel before going across to Holland and knew it well.

After checking into the hotel, I washed and decided to go down to have a look in the lobby to see if there was anybody there I knew. The first person I saw, and the last person I expected to see was Jannie and to my amazement she was dressed in the uniform of a paratrooper complete with the parachute wing on her red beret. I gave her a big hug and a kiss and suggested that we go into the bar and have a drink. She had seen the surprised look on my face when I first saw her and started to tell me how she had become a paratrooper. She explained that after I had gone to Germany, there was very little for her to do. Bert was handling most of the communications with London, so she decided to try to slip across to the other side of the river to where the Allies were. Pete de Beer had managed to do this a few weeks before. She too managed to escape and was taken to Kas de Graaf who was stationed in

Eindhoven. He asked her right away if she was prepared to be dropped back into enemy occupied territory. She agreed and within a week was at the parachute school. She was then sent to Scotland and had the same training as I had received the previous year. She was given the rank of second lieutenant, but by the time she had finished her training the war was practically over, so here she was staying in the same hotel. I was speechless and kept staring at her in disbelief. I then realized that it was now almost eleven months since I had been arrested and sent to Germany and that I knew nothing about the situation in Rotterdam during that time.

Jannie told me that Pete de Beer had also gone to the parachute school and completed the training in Scotland; he was staying in the same hotel and we would probably see him later. We had a few more drinks while she brought me up to date with the happenings in Rotterdam. Shortly after I left Rotterdam they arrested Arnold and Didi who both landed in a prison in The Hague; Didi had been released after a few weeks. Boy was still in Holland and Jannie's mother had not been well but was getting better. Then, just as Jannie had predicted, in walked second lieutenant Pete de Beer, with a big grin on his face when he saw me. Then Winny arrived, a F.A.N.Y.[89] based with the SOE, whom I had met in London before

---

8

First Aid Nurses Yeomanry. A lot of the Fany's joined the S.O.E in the beginning of WW2. These women worked on coding and signals, acted as conductors for agents and provided administration and technical support for the Special Training Schools. Their work was top secret and often highly skilled. Members operated in several theatres of war including North Africa, Italy, India and the Far East.

leaving for Holland and who had taught me how to code and decode.

Everyone wanted to know how I had fared in Germany, but I was in no mood to talk about it at that moment. Soon we all moved to the dining room and decided after dinner to go to a nightclub. It was long after midnight before I was back in my room and into bed; it took a long time to fall asleep and my mind was whirling with the news and happenings I had learned about during the evening. So, it was close to noon before I got up the next morning. Finally after a shower and a shave, I got dressed, went downstairs and headed straight for the bar where I joined Pete and Jannie who were already having a drink. I ordered one for myself and a short while later Peter said that he had a date and left. There was a moment of silence before Jannie suddenly said: 'Why don't we get married?' I was stunned and all I could say was: 'Get married? Why?' 'I just think we should! We have always been such good friends that I think that we would make a good couple.' Agreeing that we were good friends, I still questioned why we should rush into a marriage rather than wait till we were both sure. She replied that she was sure and now was as good a time as any. Why wait? I was still unconvinced but, not knowing what else to say, the idea was starting to appeal to me. So I said, 'Sure, why not?'

We had many more drinks that day. Actually it seemed that we had many drinks, often too many, every day. We had been deprived of so many things that would normally be part of the life of people growing up in their late teens or early twenties that we wanted to make up for what we had missed. It was a strange unreal time in many ways for our group of friends.

A week later Jannie and I were married with all the BBO[10] agents of the Dutch Special Forces who happened to be present in London. Neither of us even thought of going on a honeymoon and instead, we had another party. Again, everybody had way too much to drink and it was almost dawn before we got to bed. I have no recollection of the weeks that followed; they seemed to consist of one continuous party where everybody had way too much to drink. I woke up in my own bed every day not having the foggiest idea of how I got there. I can only think in retrospect that all the partying and drinking were the release of many years of tension, or perhaps the desire to make up for all those years without fun, or both.

Jannie and I saw each other very little those days except during the parties and we seemed to live life as if we had never been married. One day, I suggested that we have lunch together; it was the first time since our wedding that we had sat together quietly and were able to discuss things. I said that I thought that our marriage was a major mistake, and asked if she agreed? She did and added that she wished that we had left it the way it was, we were always such good friends and got along very well. I felt exactly the same way, but there was nothing we could do about it than and we decided to wait till we got back to Holland and resolve the situation.

Suddenly once more I had the same warm feeling for Jannie I always had before we got married. Since our wedding I had subconsciously tried to avoid

---

[10] Bureau Bizondere Opdrachten – Dutch Special Forces

her and maybe she had been trying to avoid me too. Living as husband and wife did not seem to come easy after having been such good friends for a long time. I felt like giving her a big hug now that we were back to being just friends again. Instead I said: 'Let's eat!'

When Jannie told her parents, they were furious. First, they were furious that we had got married without telling them beforehand and second, that we had decided to get divorced. Jannie's father was livid. When I think back on this episode I have to agree that it was a crazy thing to do; but after the war we were far from normal and we all did the craziest things. Most of us got it out of our system after a few months, but it took some of us longer than others. Some of the underground workers never did get back to normal, with the odd one landing in jail or in a psychiatric institute. Those who could not adjust to normal life could not seem to comprehend that it was no longer acceptable to raid a bank or distribution office and consequently it got them into very serious trouble.

During this post war period, Kas de Graaf had opened an office in the city of Utrecht. When we went back to Holland after a few weeks in London we reported to him. He had confiscated several houses in the vicinity of his office that had been occupied by German officers or by members of the Dutch National Socialist party. Some of the agents went back immediately to civilian life but I along with several others decided to stay on and work for Kas who was trying to track down those agents who had been arrested during the war and who had not yet returned. Those of us who worked for Kas were assigned one of the confiscated houses. In fact Jannie and I lived in the same house, but we hardly saw each other during the next few months.

Living conditions were still pretty grim in Holland. There was now plenty of food but many of the daily necessities were still not available; bicycle tires and tubes, clothes, shoes, toothpaste, and cigarettes were hard to find. If you had any work done, people would ask to be paid with a few cigarettes rather than with money. I told Kas that I wanted to make a few trips to London, mainly to buy things for friends and relatives. He said that any time I wanted to go he would give me a travel pass. So each time I made a trip I came back loaded with all kinds of goods. I could buy a box of a thousand cigarettes at the army supply store to be sent to a military address overseas for about thirty shillings, the equivalent of about three Canadian dollars today. Each time I was in London I would buy about ten boxes and have them sent to my military address in Holland. By the time I got back to Utrecht they were usually there waiting for me.

While I was in Holland I went to the officer's club in the evening almost every day; the liquor was cheap and plentiful. At some point I was no longer enjoying it anymore; I longed for something else yet not knowing exactly what I wanted. Then, one day in August, Kas called us all into the office and read us a letter that he had just received from SOE headquarters. They needed people with our war experience for their operations in the Far East where the war against Japan was still raging. They would be based in Ceylon. The question was who was interested? Almost everybody signed on and the very next day we were picked up at the marine airbase north of The Hague to go to England. I was very excited at the prospect of going to

Ceylon and joining the fighting forces again. I had had enough of the partying and drinking and was looking forward to going to that part of the world close to where my parents had lived all these years. It was more than five years since I had heard from them.

Chapter Fourteen

Sri Lanka with Force 136 (Covert Espionage and Sabotage)

The plane was waiting for us when we arrived at the airbase the next day. I could not believe my eyes when I saw the interior of the plane; it was very luxurious with easy chairs around tables rather than the usual seats. The pilot officer who was there to welcome us explained that this was the private plane of Air Vice-Marshall Tedder who had insisted that his plane was sent to pick us up. The short trip over was made even more pleasant because we could help ourselves to drinks at the bar.

At the base where we landed, the luxury came to an abrupt halt. We were assigned cots in one of the Quonset huts and told that we would get all the necessary vaccinations the next day and probably leave for Ceylon almost immediately. The next day turned out to be sheer hell. Right after breakfast we were told to go to the medical building. The doctor gave us a cursory examination and told us to proceed to the next room where we received the required inoculations, a great many of them, including: smallpox, sleeping sickness, typhoid, cholera, tetanus, plus a few that I had never heard of before.

We were directed to the soccer field after the medical and inoculations, where we were kept jogging, running, playing soccer, anything to keep us on the move. We were told that exercise would 'get the stuff that they pumped into us moving through our system'. After a few hours of this activity I felt like I was going to die and wanted nothing more than to go to bed and sleep. There was not a chance, because the field was fenced off and the gate was kept closed. If we just sat on the grass we were told to get up and keep moving. Finally they gave us a break for lunch. Most of us wanted to go to bed after lunch and sneaked out to the bunkhouse only to find it locked! When we finally did get to bed we were totally exhausted.

The next morning we boarded a York, one of the largest planes flying at that time that would take us to Ceylon. We flew non-stop to Aden and most of us, still tired from the day before, just slept the whole time. Finally, we could feel by the pressure on our ears that we were descending but when I looked out of the window, all I could see were pinkish grey clouds. Then, the wheels were on the ground but we could still barely see anything. We had landed in Aden in the middle of a sandstorm. As soon as the door was opened we were told we should proceed as fast as possible to the mess hall where we would be served a meal; the plane would be refuelled and we would be leaving as soon as possible. We were advised to breathe through our handkerchiefs and protect our eyes as much as possible. Sand was everywhere; it was very fine and found its way through minute cracks into the dining room where we had lunch and into the kitchen. We had our meal and waited about twenty minutes before we boarded the plane. I could see out of the window army personnel who were working outside in hundred and ten degree heat with sand whirling around them. I was very glad that I was not stationed there! After boarding our plane again, the pilot lost no time in starting the engines and getting airborne again. We were all very relieved to get above the sand and back into the clean air.

It was close to midnight before we landed next in Karachi in what is now Pakistan. We were bussed to the place where we were to stay for the night that consisted of a huge camp with tents as far as the eye could see. When we reported to the office, we were each given a tent number together with a map indicating its approximate location. We also received a towel, a piece of soap, shaving material, and bedding. However, finding my tent in the sparsely lit camp was no easy task but I finally did find it with the help of a little Indian boy, who followed me inside and told me that he would look after me. He offered to show me where I could shower while he made up my bed. I took off my clothes, wrapped a towel around me, and went to have a shower. The nice cold water felt wonderful and I stayed in the shower for quite a while appreciating the boy's help. When I returned to my tent, the little boy had disappeared with my wallet, my change and my bag with all my personal belongings. I ran outside to see if I could spot him, but of course he was long gone and was probably waiting at a safe distance for his next customer after disposing of his loot. Realizing the futility of trying to do something about it, I went to bed and was soon sound asleep.

When I woke up the next morning, I got dressed and went to the office to report the boy. Apparently they were helpless to solve the problem. They tried to keep them out of the camp but they still manage to sneak into the compound under the cover of darkness and do their dirty work. The camp was only patrolled at the boundaries, and once inside the thieves pretty much had a free hand. Resigned to my losses, I left for the dining room to have breakfast. Most of the gang was already there and one of the crewmembers who sat at the same table told us that we would probably be on our way to Ceylon within a few hours. I told him of my experience with the little boy. He was not surprised and said that this happened quite frequently. He suggested that next time a boy welcomed me into my tent I should just grab him by the neck and take him to the office. I wished I had known!

We hung around in the comfort of the air-conditioned dining room until we boarded the plane and by ten o'clock we were airborne again and landed several hours later at Colombo airport. We were bussed from the airport to a large camp about thirty miles out of Colombo in the middle of nowhere. Once inside the gate we were told that this was a high security area surrounded by five strands of rolled barbed wire and guarded by Ghurkhas twenty-four hours a day every hundred feet all through the camp. We were advised to adhere strictly to the security rules that would be made known to us during the next few days. In the meantime we were to stay within the confines of the camp. It had its own completely equipped little hospital with nurses, a doctor, and a small pharmacy.

We were now part of 'Force 136', a unit that was involved with covert, espionage and sabotage operations in enemy occupied territory.[11] It all sounded very familiar! The large camp also encompassed a smaller unit which housed the offices, radio

---

[11] The first time I heard 'Force 136' referred to after the war was in the movie 'Bridge on the River Kwai'. In the movie they referred to it as 'Force 163' with headquarters at the Mount Lavinia Hotel just outside the City of Colombo. Hollywood version of Force 136!

equipment, and sleeping quarters of about a dozen members of the (SOE) F.A.N.Y., who maintained wireless operations between the camp and the numerous parties operating within enemy territory and in fact had nothing to do with nursing. Their little compound was out of bounds to everybody else.

The bunkhouses had either two or four beds, officers were assigned one with two beds and NCOs were housed four to a bunkhouse. There was a strict regimen in the camp with wake-up call at six and by a quarter after six we had to be assembled at the starting point of our thirty minutes run. An actual roll call was held and if you were absent you were sent for and received a stern reprimand from the officer in charge in front of the full assembly. This happened only once the first day and after that we all made sure to be there on time. After a while we realized that the run did wonders for our system, especially after drinking too much the night before. About ten minutes into the run we could feel the perspiration pouring down our bodies and it felt great. Everyone jumped into the shower after the run and the cool water felt wonderful.

We were divided into groups of three or four and each group was assigned a certain operation. Our group was slated to be landed by submarine on the north coast of the island of Sumatra. We were supplied with very detailed maps of the landing area and the surrounding terrain. I was to be in charge of the group and for the next few days we went over all the details of the area. I was the only one of our group of four who could speak Malay, the language of almost the entire group of islands now called Indonesia, but I had not spoken the language since I left for Holland in 1939 so my Malay was a bit rusty. Fortunately there were some

Ambonese soldiers in the camp who could speak only Malay and I was able to practice with them.

A short time later I was made the 'wines officer,' which meant that I was now in charge of all the liquor in the camp and responsible for its distribution. Officers were entitled to one bottle of whiskey, one bottle of gin, and two bottles of sherry every month at no expense, but they had to pay for anything over and above this allowance. Many officers did not want any of their allowance so that these bottles were available for sale to others.

It became obvious to me that the men, including the Ambonese, were getting bored due to prolonged inactivity so I went to the commanding officer to speak about this and he suggested that I take them on patrol in the surrounding area. I selected a group of eight men including a fellow officer, Lee Faber. The others were two NCOs and four Ambonese soldiers. We got together the necessary tents and food for ten days and left the camp. Two army trucks took us to a spot about three miles away and dropped us off on the bank of a river, and would pick us up again at the same spot in ten days.

We set up camp next to the river in the shade of a couple of huge trees. It was the dry season and most of the riverbed was dry with a pocket of water every hundred yards or so. We soon discovered that these pockets were teeming with fish. Whenever we decided to have fish for our meal, we would throw a hand grenade in the water and about thirty seconds after the explosion a lot of fish would float to the surface. All we had to do was to jump in the water and throw the fish on the bank before they regained consciousness and swam back down again since the explosion would only stun them for a few minutes.

Every second day we would break camp and move to a different spot along the river close to a pool of water. One day, just after we jumped into the water to retrieve the fish after an explosion we were surprised by the sudden appearance of a crocodile that happened to be in the same body of water. We were out of the water in no time and a safe distance away from the bank! Apparently that crocodile usually slept just below a very steep portion of the bank and so we decided to blow him up. We attached explosive to the primer and the primer cord and used the cord to lower the explosive next to the crocodile that seemed to be fast asleep, at least he was not moving. We stood back and detonated the charge and when we peered over the bank, we saw that the crocodile had been blown to pieces. That night I woke up to a foul odour and wondered if it was caused by the decomposing pieces of crocodile. The next morning the odour was very strong and there was no doubt of the cause. It was almost unbearable and we decided to move camp a distance upwind.

Lee and I decided that we should go on a boar hunt and if we could not find any boar towards the evening perhaps to hunt for a tiger. We left at noon with two of the soldiers who were familiar with the terrain. We more or less followed the river as the area where we were most likely to find animals. Sure enough, we came upon a large herd of elephants standing up to their bellies in the water and spraying each other with water. It was a fascinating spectacle and we watched them for quite a while from behind a tree until they decided to move, fortunately away from us.   It was getting dark, so we decided to start walking towards our camp. Then, in the light of our flashlight we saw a pair of big green eyes, unmistakably those of a tiger. We backed away slowly and I raised my rifle with the intention of shooting but one of the guides quietly raised the barrel of my gun and told me not to shoot. Seconds later the glowing eyes slowly turned away followed by the huge body of the tiger and disappeared into the dense forest. We were not sure what the tiger was going to do, perhaps it might attack us from a different direction! So we stayed where we were and scanned the area all around. After about five minutes, it seemed that the tiger had left the area so we started to hike home. When I asked the guide why he stopped me shooting at the tiger, he explained that it was too dark to get an accurate shot. He added that you need to hit a tiger in one of his eyes, otherwise the bullet would not penetrate but ricochet off his head, and then the tiger would attack for sure! He could have made mincemeat of the four of us and I was glad that I had followed the soldier's advice! At the end of ten days, we broke camp and returned to the agreed pick-up spot. It felt good to get back to base and be able to have a proper shower and sleep in a regular bed again, but we had all enjoyed the change.

Ceylon, 1945

Ceylon, with Lee and a native guide

Chapter Fifteen

A Strange Offer, the Atom Bomb Ends the War, and a Wedding in Colombo

I had met and become friends with a two naval officers who were stationed in Colombo on one of the largest ocean recovery ships in the harbour. We quite often went out together in the evening and I spent some time with them on board their ship in the harbour and was able to get information about the ships that were coming in, including Dutch troop transport ships that came from the Dutch East Indies carrying Dutch people back to Holland. These people had been in a Japanese prison camp all during the war. When one of these ships was in the harbour I usually went on board to see if there were any of the passengers that I knew; I would ask to see the passenger list to see if perhaps my parents or my sister was on board.

One day I was approached by an army colonel who told me that some people were interested in talking to me. He did not know why they wanted to meet me but I was asked to meet them for lunch at the officer's club the next day. When I entered the officers' club, I was met by two high-ranking Army officers and we sat down at a table in the corner of the dining room. After some small talk, they came straight to the point and asked me if I would be willing to train guerrilla units in China. I would be paid ten thousand pounds upon signing and the money would be deposited in a bank in my name. The contract would be for one year and during that year I would be supplied with the necessary funds. I was silent for a while letting the proposal sink in. Then I asked who these guerrillas were supposed to be fighting? The response was 'Tsiang Kai Tsek.' This reply astounded me since he was supposed to be our ally and, besides that, he was my hero. I told them I would never support anyone who was supposed to fight him. They immediately told me to forget that I had ever seen them and got up and left before we had even ordered a drink. I stayed by myself, ordered a drink and had lunch. I kept pondering the proposition and wondered why the British would support people fighting Tsiang Kai Tsek while he was the ally of the United States during the war. It was very strange and I could not understand it.

There was a large WREN camp, two ATS camps, and one small WAAF camp in Colombo. I asked somebody how I could arrange a date with one of the girls, apparently all I had to do was to go to one of the camps, ask to see the person in charge and tell her that I was looking for a date. I liked the girls in a navy uniform the best so one day I went to the WREN camp and did as had been suggested. It was arranged that my date would join me the next evening and I would take her out for dinner and dancing afterwards and I would pick her up shortly after five. All the WRENS liked to dance and enjoyed being asked for a date, but the camp liked to see the girls return to base before midnight! It certainly seemed so simple.

When I arrived at the camp the next day I was met by the person I had seen the day before who led me into a reception room. There she introduced me to eight girls and three male officers who were there for the same reason as me. I chose a girl and asked her if she would like to come for dinner with me and perhaps go on to a dance afterwards. She said she would love to and we left. Her name was Sheila and she turned out to be a terrific dancer. We went out dancing many more times after that first evening and we even participated in a local dance contest in which we won the first prize in the 'slow waltz' and second prize in the 'foxtrot'; not bad for a pair of amateurs, especially since there were quite a few advanced dancers in the competition.

There had still been no word about our mission when on August 6, 1945 the atom bomb was dropped on Hiroshima followed a few days later by another on Nagasaki, putting an end to the war, almost six years after it started! A feeling of happiness at the war ending overwhelmed me, yet at the same time wondered what life would be like in peacetime. I felt as if I was suddenly in a totally different world, a world without war, one that I had forgotten and never really known as an adult. I was thinking about the many thousands of men, including the many prisoners of war, who would soon be going home. Most of the restrictions in our camp were lifted, and we no longer had to sign in and out when leaving the camp.

On the day the Japanese admitted defeat, Colombo broke out into one big party that went on till the early morning hours. Many of the men who had arrived here at the same time as me went home as soon as possible. I decided to wait because I wanted to return to Holland by boat, preferably the same boat that my mother, my dad, or my sister was on. Another reason was I was having so much fun in Colombo. I stayed most of the time in the Mount Lavinia Hotel, right on the ocean a few miles from Colombo. The day usually started with a swim in the ocean at daybreak when the water was still calm. By ten o'clock the big waves started to come in and I usually spent the rest of the day surfing with only a short break for lunch.

One of the men in the camp, van Lienden was also from Holland, and before the war he had been the table tennis champion of Holland, and one of the twenty best tennis players in the country. He would also have represented Holland in sailing at an international sailing competition that was never held because of the war. He had gained entry to the Royal Colombo Yacht Club and participated in an ocean race every Sunday, sailing in one of the boats that belonged to the club. He asked me if I wanted to be his second man and I readily accepted. He certainly was a master sailor and we won the race every Sunday; he knew exactly how to get ahead of another boat and how to prevent a boat from passing us. Although I loved to sail, I did not particularly enjoy his company. He never spoke a word except to tell me to mind the jib if the edge happened to be slightly fluttering, or to let me know that he was going to tack. Throughout the race he was totally focussed and watching the other boats. When I first met him he invited me to a game of table tennis, which was not much fun either because I never managed to get even one point against him. Every single game ended with a twenty-one to zero score. So pretty soon I declined to play with him anymore, and then I found out that no-one else in the camp wanted to play with him for the same reason.

One morning, while on my early morning swim I decided to go way out because it was nice and calm and the sun was about to come over the horizon. When I decided that I was out far enough I looked to one side and spotted the dorsal fin of a huge shark. I immediately turned around and, on my back, slowly swam to the shore while keeping an eye on the shark. I had been told that one should always try to keep the white inside of your hands and the bottom of your feet facing away from the shark and to avoid looking exhausted. The shark was circling me but I knew that as soon as the water between me and the shore became too shallow he would no longer complete the circle and would stay in the deeper water. Imagine my relief when he disappeared; I had been in the water long enough and I went ashore. It had been an interesting experience!

There were two Dutch Force 136 female officers in the camp. One of them, Rita, had been in training in England at the same time as Jannie. One of the Dutch officers, Frank Ledeboer, had proposed to Rita and the wedding was to be held at the City Hall in Colombo. Rita asked me and Peter Tazelaar, another friend to be witnesses. On the day of the wedding, which was to be at eleven in the morning, Peter and I decided to have a drink and opened a bottle of whiskey. Fifteen minutes before the ceremony one of us realized we had better get to the city hall; we hopped in a cab and got there just in time, slightly inebriated I might add! Once we were seated, the clerk of the court started the ceremony, but none of us could understand a word he said. At that point I decided to take over, I asked the clerk to stop and went to the other side of the table and told the clerk that I was going to perform the ceremony. He looked a little surprised but got up, gave me his chair and sat opposite the bride and groom. So it was that I performed the wedding ceremony, from beginning to end; I am not sure if it was legal! I got up, went to the other side of the table again and kissed the bride. Bride and groom then stayed for a while to sign the necessary documents and receive the wedding certificate while we waited outside in the hall. We all went to the officer's mess for lunch; and that is the last thing I remember of that day!

I had been checking regularly with the harbour master's office to see if any ships from the Dutch East Indies were due in. If one were expected I would go to the harbour to wait for it and then go on board to check the passenger list to see if any members of my family were on board. A few days following the wedding, I received a letter from my mother! I stared at it in disbelief, but there it was, addressed to me, in care of Force 136, Colombo in the familiar handwriting! I opened it and it soon became clear how she knew that I was here. A contingent of British officers had gone to Djakarta and my sister happened to meet one of them. When he heard her name, he said that there was a Mulholland in Ceylon where he had just come from, maybe her brother? They compared a few notes and she decided that it had to be me, ran home and told my Mom. What an incredible coincidence! My mother wrote to tell me that my sister Elsa would be boarding a ship soon to go to Holland, and she would be following several months later. She and my sister had been in a Japanese camp and my Dad also, but in a camp for men. They had been reunited only a couple of weeks ago. Of course she had no idea where I had been or what I had been doing during the war. When I wrote back to her, I decided to tell her only that I was in the military and hoped to go back to Holland soon and get out of the army. I also told her that I was planning to return on the same ship as my sister.

The ship arrived about a week after I sent my letter. When I came on board and looked through the passenger list, there was her name, Elsa Mulholland. I asked the steward to call on the intercom for her to come to the steward's office. When she arrived and saw me she gasped. Seeing me was a total surprise because my letter had arrived after she left. I tried to book a berth at the purser's office, but was told that I better see the captain and after a bit of talking I managed to book a berth. When the captain told me he would be able to provide better accommodation than a bunk for an officer, I assured him that this was not necessary and I was sure there were hundreds of women on board who would love to 'upgrade' their bunk to something better. I went back to shore, packed my bags, said good bye to my navy friends and came back on board, this time for good and on my way to Holland. We left that same night.

Chapter Sixteen

Going Home, Getting Divorced, Re-connecting with Normal Life

The ship we were sailing on used to be Dutch passenger ship before the war during which it had been converted to a troopship. I did not relish the thought of sleeping anywhere inside and planned to string up my army issue hammock somewhere on deck and sleep inside only during bad weather. The hammock was made for the tropics complete with roof and mosquito netting all around, and in fact I was able to sleep on deck for the entire trip. I spent the first few days with my sister and learning from her how things had been for her and my parents during the war. My parents had been separated for the duration of the war, but had been reunited about a week after the armistice. My sister and my mother had been together all during the war. Conditions were not now that rosy at home; the indigenous population were not prepared to let the Dutch take over the reins again and wanted their independence. The Dutch population had to be protected by the soldiers who were mostly British, and it would several months before the British would be replaced by Dutch troops. The mostly Dutch passengers on the ship had been interned in camps during the war and it was quite obvious that, like my sister, they had all suffered from malnutrition. Elsa wanted to know about my war experience, and how it was that I came to be in Colombo. They had assumed that I was still in Holland only to discover that I was in Ceylon when they had talked to the British soldier.

Obviously I was going to have to tell her the whole story when we had time.

The first evening when I went to the first class lounge, there were no passengers in the lounge except for a few British officers I had not seen before. I was somewhat puzzled till I saw a sign on the entrance door that said: 'British Officers Only'. It seemed to me to be a very large lounge for a handful of British officers, and on a Dutch ship to boot! I approached a group of officers having a drink and asked where I could find the commanding officer. I found the CO in his cabin and motioning me to sit down asked why I wanted to see him. I asked him who had made the rule that the first class lounge was only for British officers. He told me that he had, before the passengers boarded in Djakarta. When I asked for the reason, he just looked at me without replying. I told him that I did not think he had the right to do this! The people he was excluding had all spent several years in a Japanese camp and should not be denied the few luxuries the ship had to offer. I told him to remove the sign immediately and have the captain or one of the ship's officers make an announcement over the intercom, in Dutch, that the lounge would from now on be open to all passengers. Outwardly I stayed icy calm but inwardly I was boiling. He must have sensed that I was dead serious and agreed immediately; although he had the rank of major he decided not to argue. I got up and left and within fifteen minutes the announcement came over the intercom.

There were a lot of young women on board between the ages of sixteen and twenty who had been in camp at a time when they were teenagers and who normally would have started taking dancing lessons, going to school dances, etc. But these youngsters had never learned to dance; this fact became very obvious a few days later when somebody organized a dance. As there was no live band on board, the music was provided by a record player. When the music began there were only a few middle-aged people on the floor and some of the young girls who could scrape together enough courage were trying to dance with each other. I spotted one lady who looked to be a very good dancer and at the first opportunity I asked her for a dance. She had been a dance teacher, and after dancing with her several more times that evening, she told me that she had thought she would offer to teach the young girls to dance and asked me if I would consider being her partner. I readily agreed and from then on until the end of the voyage we taught dancing. It was very gratifying to see the girls as well as the boys and young men enjoying themselves with their newfound skills. Some of them became very good dancers indeed!

As we passed through the Suez Canal, my thoughts returned to 1939 and how it had been then. Here I was again under such very different circumstances. We laid over in Suez for one day and this gave me the opportunity to go to the army supply store to pick up a new battle dress and other clothing. My old uniform had started to look a bit worn, but when I changed into my new one I was almost sorry that I was not wearing the old one which felt so very comfortable! I decided to keep the old one as a spare. The rest of the voyage went without incident. This time I would not disembark at Marseilles but sail through the Strait of Gibraltar and on to Amsterdam.

As we approached the coast of Holland and entered the inlet leading towards the Noordzee Canal I stood on the bow of the ship and looked down on the small houses and the people on the street who were waving at the passengers they knew were coming back from the Dutch East Indies. From my vantage point Holland seemed to lay there at my feet and I was totally overcome with emotion. I remained rooted at the bow during the rest of the way through the Noordzee canal to Amsterdam looking at the countryside around me and thinking back on the past few years. The horrific things that took place in Europe and the Far East during the war years and I felt gratified that the war was finally over. And yet, I also thought about the thousands of human lives that had been lost and the horrible and senseless destruction of the landscape and the many cities. It seemed like a horrible nightmare with a happy ending, if there is such a thing. As we approached the pier I could see hundreds of people on the quay who were there to welcome their relatives, friends, and quite possibly their special loved ones whom they expected to be on the ship. More and more passengers had now joined me on the bow in order to get a closer look at the crowd, but as the ship came closer to the quay most of them left to get ready to disembark.

As soon as the gangplanks were lowered throngs of people left the ship and were reunited with their friends and relatives. My sister was going to go with a friend who was being picked up by her relatives with whom they were going to stay. I said good-bye to her and gave her a phone number where she could get in touch with me. I went and gathered my belongings, disembarked, took a streetcar to the railroad station, and boarded the train for Utrecht.

The train to Utrecht was one that stopped at every little town and what would normally have taken about thirty minutes took more than an hour. But I enjoyed the slower journey, looking at the countryside that showed signs of getting back to normal. I struck up a conversation with my neighbour who told me that some food items such as sugar, beef, and liquor were still in short supply, but that generally things were not so bad.

In Utrecht I took a cab to the BBO[12] office and found Kas and his secretary Dorothy whom he had married. Most of the boys had got their demobilization papers and had more or less returned to civilian life; jobs, however, were still hard to come by. He was in the process of winding down the office and writing his final report before closing down. I asked him where Jannie was and he said that she also had shed her uniform and was staying with her parents in Hillegersberg. We spent the rest of the afternoon talking and then the three of us had dinner and kept on talking. There was a lot of news to catch up on, as I had been away for almost eight months.

Most of the wartime 'bigwigs' had been arrested and were behind bars. One surprising revelation was that the head of the Army Intelligence in Holland, Major Giskes, was free pending further investigations. Apparently his activities had been absolutely clean during the war, he had never committed any atrocities, and had tried to keep the agents out of the hands of the Gestapo, the Sicherheits Dienst, and other authorities knowing that they would either end up in a concentration camp or be unceremoniously shot. His

---

[12] Bureau Special Assignments, Netherlands section of the Special Force

boss, Admiral Canaris, the chief of the German Intelligence, had been hanged by Hitler, suspected of being part of the failed assassination attempt. Much later it was revealed that at one point during the war, Canaris had turned against Hitler and from then on had done everything in his power to assist the Allies mainly by withholding critical information long enough to be of no use to Hitler's staff.

I asked Kas if there was anything else that he wanted me to do. There was nothing, but before giving me my demobilization papers, he wanted me to go to London to see a person whose name he would give me the following day. I agreed to go as soon as possible without having the foggiest idea what this was all about. Kas gave me no further information. I took a plane to London the next day and arranged to meet the person whose name Kas had given me in the lobby of the Cumberland Hotel close to the entrance to the dining room. I would recognize him as he would be holding a green coloured book in his left hand. We met and he introduced himself as 'John Inglis' with the rank of colonel; we agreed to have a drink and then lunch, my previous experiences convinced me that this was not his real name. The fact that I did not meet him in his office was also indicated that he was involved with the secret service, probably MI5, and I was curious to discover the reason for this meeting. I soon found out. He offered me a position with the British Intelligence overseas. I would be immediately elevated to the rank of major and probably be posted to Turkey, working out of the embassy. Up to this point I had just listened, not saying a word, but I replied that I wanted to think about it for a while. Several thoughts and emotions passed through my mind; on the one hand the idea appealed to me but then I started to wonder if I really wanted this sort of life now the war was over. So far everything I had done was because I wanted to defeat the enemy, but did I want to continue this life of cloak and dagger in peacetime?

Then I knew my answer. I said 'I think that at this point I want to be away from this type of business and now that the war is over just live a normal life. The offer is very attractive but my answer is, No, thank you. The subject was closed and on finishing our luncheon we parted ways and he said goodbye and wished me good luck. I took a cab to the airport and a plane back to Holland.

I saw Kas the next morning and told him about my meeting and asked him for my demobilization papers. He said that he would have them ready for me in a couple of days so I decided to use the time to go and see Jannie in Hillegersberg. I phoned the familiar number and it was Jannie who answered the phone. She said she would prefer to come on the train to Utrecht and see me there. She asked if I was staying in 'our' house, the house assigned to us as married couple when Kas set up offices in Utrecht. When Jannie arrived at the house a couple of hours later we kissed but both felt awkward. I cursed the fact that we had got married. We had always been so easy and free with each other, such good friends but our marriage seemed to have put an end to this wonderful relationship.

I asked her why she was not keen to have me visit her in Hillegersberg; she told me that her Dad was so mad at me that he never wanted to see me again. Jannie's Mom would dearly love to see me but her hands were tied, and Boy never argued with his Dad. Her Mom sent her love and wished me all the best for the future; she realized that we had made a mistake and that it was up to us to deal with it. I had suspected that this was behind her reluctance to have me come to Hillegersberg and felt sorry that this was the way my relationship with the Sissingh family had ended. But, so be it, there was nothing I could do about it.

Jannie told me that as far as she knew, the only way open to us was for her to file for divorce on the grounds of adultery and then, when it got to court, for me not contest it. She did not feel at all good about it charging me with adultery! She said we had only two options, I could charge her or she could charge me with adultery, and I certainly did not want to do that. We decided to act as soon as possible and to move to an apartment in The Hague as the office in Utrecht was about to be closed down. It was truly amazing how the awkwardness we felt with each other seemed to disappear as soon as we decided to get a divorce. We felt as if we were no longer married but friends again and quite comfortable with each other.

When Kas gave me my demobilization papers I told him of our plans and asked if there was a car he could let us have in the meantime. He told me that the best ones had been picked by the men, who had left before me, but there were still two left and to choose the one I wanted. I said goodbye to him and Dorothy and went to choose my car. The cars had been confiscated from the Germans immediately after the war; we had all been using them and had more or less claimed them for ourselves. I went to where he told me I would find the cars and I saw that they had indeed been picked over! The mechanic said that neither of them was very good but that the Ford Anglia was probably the better of the two. I started it up and drove it away; at least it seemed to work!

Jannie and I packed our belongings in the car and drove to The Hague. Houses to rent were plentiful so we just drove around looking for 'house for rent' signs till we found a suitable house, signed up, paid the first month's rent and moved in. It was only partially furnished house but as long as there were two beds, some tables and chairs, it was fine with us. It was fairly large and in a nice part of the city.

The following morning Jannie went to see a lawyer about filing the divorce papers. It would take about a month before it came up in court, and during this time we saw little of each other during the day. I was busy finalizing my demobilization and did a lot of walking exploring the city and enjoying the people; it was so pleasant to see the people laughing again and going freely about their business. I purposely dressed in civilian clothes during the day so that I attracted no undue attention.

One of the papers that Kas had given me entitled me to buy clothes, but I had to take it to a government office in order to get the coupons that entitled me to buy the different pieces of attire. A young military recruit manned the reception desk at the government office. I stood in front of his desk for a while and when he finally looked up, he said something like, 'And what do you want?' I literally blew up and shouted, 'Stand at attention! You had better learn how to talk to people, otherwise you don't belong here. You happen to be talking to Captain Mulholland!'

The young man sprang to attention and stammered; 'Yes sir, I am sorry sir' or words to that effect. His commanding officer, a young lieutenant, came to the front, introduced himself and asked me to come into his office. I was still fuming mad at the man at the desk and gave him a stern look. He still stood at attention and looked mighty scared. The lieutenant apologized and said that he would give him a good reprimand and remove him from the front desk, at least until he had learned how to properly address people. I suggested that this was probably a good lesson for everybody else in the office too. The lieutenant agreed and asked me if there was anything he could do for me. I showed him my papers and told him that I had come to pick up my coupons for my clothing ration. He checked them and once more apologized for the way I had been treated by the man at the reception desk; he would tell everybody in the office to be courteous to every person that walks into this office. He added that most of the men were young recruits on their first jobs. They still had a lot to learn and must recognize that they were dealing with ex military personnel who had fought in the war and who were certainly not prepared to tolerate any lip from a young recruit. He then gave me a handful of coupons, permits, etc., apologizing that this was all he could do for me. I checked the papers, thanked him and left. As I passed the reception desk, the young man jumped up and saluted; I acknowledged his salute and walked out of the building.

It was June 1946 and the day of the divorce hearing. Jannie had gone to the courthouse early in the morning and was going to phone me as soon as the hearing was over. Shortly before noon she called with the news 'We are just friends again!' We decided to celebrate, by having dinner at the officers' club and then went on to have a night on the town. We had a ball, we danced and we laughed and didn't go home till three in the morning, totally exhausted. We had been married for almost a year to the day.

A few days later we served notice on the house we had rented and I found a nice apartment in Scheveningen, close to the ocean and within a few blocks of the streetcar, and within a week I moved in to my new home. Jannie had moved out a few days earlier and was going to stay at her parents' home for a while.

Chapter Seventeen

Finding a Job and Meeting Anna and receiving the Order of the Bronze Lion from Queen Wilhelmina.

Now I had to start looking for a job as my regular army pay would soon stop, and the lump sum of money paid to me after I returned to Holland would not last forever. I was not very keen on getting a job in Holland, so I decided to go to the only international company I could think of which was the Shell Oil Company that had its headquarters in The Hague.

The Shell building was huge occupying almost an entire city block. I got a job application form from the man in the information booth and took it home to complete. It was easy to fill in, and the one question which was really appealing to me and which I answered with an unequivocal 'YES' was: 'Will you accept employment overseas?' I went back to the Shell building the next day and dropped off the form. This was the only application I made as all the other companies I talked to who had offices overseas before the war that, were still in the early stages of getting organized as they reopened their offices.

While waiting to hear from the Shell Oil Company, I spent my time getting re-acquainted with life in Holland where things were slowly getting back to normal. It was good to see the store shelves gradually filling again, although a lot of items were still in short supply. I still had an enormous supply of cigarettes so it was usually easy for me to buy the things I wanted in exchange for cigarettes, even without the required coupons. I also knew scores of officers who were going back and forth to England on a regular basis who were willing to buy things for me. But even in England there were shortages.

In the evenings I would usually wore my uniform to go to the officers' club for a drink and dinner. On one of those occasions I met Hank Geysen who had been dropped into Holland a few months after me to train the underground in Rotterdam. I knew him from nautical college, and we had gone to Ceylon at the same time. He was no longer in the military but, like me, put on his uniform for the occasion. We had dinner together and talked about our time in Ceylon; we had both been slated to go on a mission when the Japanese capitulated. He and his family had rented a house for the summer in Noordwijk and invited me to drop in and stay with them any time; this invitation was extended to many men like me who had spent time in Ceylon. The arrangement was very informal and everyone took care of their own meals. Not surprisingly his wife could not cook for everyone who turned up so guests usually made themselves a sandwich for lunch and often everyone went to the hotel for dinner and stayed for the dance afterwards. Noordwijk, located on the coast not far north of The Hague, used to be a very popular holiday resort so I assured him that I would visit him very soon.

After about three weeks I received instructions from Shell to report to the office for a physical examination. The doctor's office was a large room with a hardwood floor; the only pieces of furniture consisting of a large mahogany desk that was totally bare save for a desk pad, one leather chair for the doctor, and one leather chair on the other side of the desk. The doctor pointed to a small cubicle on the far side of the room and told me to get undressed. Inside was a sign that said, 'If you sleep with your socks on you may leave them on here also,' a clear indication that I was supposed to take off 'all' my clothes! When I emerged the doctor looked me over, then pointed to the empty chair across his desk and told me to sit down. It was a strange sensation to sit with my bare posterior on a cold leather chair and could not help wondering if somebody wiped the seat after every visitor!

'I understand that you want to go overseas?'

'Yes doctor, I do.'

'Are you married?'

'No doctor, I am not.'

'How is your sex life?'

I certainly had not expected a question like that and it took me a few seconds before I answered.

'I am sorry doctor but I don't think that is any of your business.'

He looked at me for a while and then said: 'You can get dressed again.'

When I came back into the room he handed me an envelope to leave at the front desk. I thanked him and left. That was the extent of my 'medical' examination. I looked at the envelope, it was stamped 'Manager Personnel'. I gave it to the person at the front desk and left.

Scheveningen was another popular seaside resort and there was always lots of activity at this time of the year. My favourite place was the dunes to the north of the city. I used to get up very early and go for a long walk in the dunes where one could walk for miles without meeting a single soul, especially at that time of the day. At night there was more going on and

I used to go out for a drink and a meal but I never stayed out very long.

I received a quick response from the Shell Oil Company that I was accepted and could start work on Monday, the first of July, 1946. Before then, I was asked to go to the office to fill out a few forms. I decided to look for accommodation closer to my work place, preferably close enough to be able to walk or bike to the office rather than having to depend on streetcars. I soon found a pleasant large room overlooking a tree-lined street bordering a grassy area beside a pond filled with all sorts of water plants including water lilies. Two days after arranging to take the room, I received a phone call from the landlady asking me if it would be possible for me to delay moving in for two weeks. Apparently a young lady had rented a room on the second floor, which would not be vacated for another two weeks; she needed a place to stay because she had just started a new job. Since there was no immediate urgency for me to move in I said that arrangement would be perfectly acceptable. There were still ten days before I started my job with Shell, and there was no reason why I could not take the streetcar for a few days.

I dropped by my new home a few days later where an attractive young lady was talking to the landlady on the sidewalk outside the house. When the landlady saw me she introduced me as the nice gentleman who was giving her his room for a few weeks. The young lady was Anna, my wife and that is how we met! [13]

---

[13] This is not the way Anna remembers it but since she does not want to give me her version , mine will stand.

Anna thanked me profusely and after exchanging a few pleasantries, I left and went to the Shell office to fill out some papers. I was told that I would be working in the purchasing department that dealt with parts for their worldwide drilling operations. I met with the head of the department and told him that I would be starting work on the first of July. He showed me around and gave me an outline of my job. It did not sound very exciting or challenging and I began to wonder how long it would be before I was sent overseas.

The first of July came all too quickly and although I did not look forward to spending my days behind a desk, I was anxious to start my new job, to start leading a normal life and to completely detach myself from the war. The working day was as I had anticipated but I decided to bite the bullet and make the best of it; after all it did give me the opportunity to learn something entirely new. However, it bored me to tears and I was looking forward to the weekend that I planned to spend at Hank's place in Noordwijk.

That first Friday evening after work I donned my uniform and went to the officer's club for dinner, where I sat at a table with three British officers. During the conversation over dinner I asked them why they were still in Holland more than a year after the end of the war. All three were involved with investigating the disappearance of art treasures from museums and private, mainly Jewish collections. I had not heard anything about disappearing treasures before and discovered that literally thousands of items had been taken from museums and collections in Holland and the other occupied countries during the war.

I rose early the next morning, put on my uniform and took the train to Leiden and then a bus from there to Noordwijk. It being still too early to go to Hank's home, I had a leisurely breakfast and walked along the beach till I was at the edge of town and then double-backed on the road to his house. There was a note on the door that said, 'Please don't ring the bell, just step in and make yourself comfortable.' Only Hank was up, everybody else was still asleep, so we chatted for a while. He told me that a high school friend of his wife, Auda, was staying with them for the weekend and they had gone to bed very late. He got his breakfast after discovering that I had already eaten and invited me to stay the weekend? Maybe we could all go to the 'Huis ter Duin' hotel for dinner and stay for the dance afterwards. I was happy to accept if his wife did not object. He reassured me that there was probably not a single day when they had no guests and most of the time more than one. A lot of the former BBO guys have come here off and on; I found out later that the neighbours had complained about seeing so many uniformed men and women going in and out at all hours of the day that they had started to think that this was a house of ill repute!

When the others got up I had another big surprise. The girl who was introduced as Auda's high school friend was Anna! We went for dinner that night and stayed for the dance at which I danced mostly with Anna. Afterwards we walked home along the beach as it was a beautiful starlit night talking mostly about what Anna did during the war. We did not kiss or even hold hands, but I think that that was when it happened: I fell in love! Anna and I went back to The Hague the next afternoon; we said good-bye and each went to our own homes. It would not be long before her room became available and I could move in to mine and we would be living in the same house.

At the office, it was more of the same and I was beginning to wonder if I had done the right thing applying for this job. But I realized that I could not continue living without a steady income and not many jobs were available. In this job I at least had the prospect of being sent overseas.

One day taking a different route home from work I discovered a complex of tennis courts and decided to see if I could join a tennis club. I saw a few people in the clubhouse and asked them about joining. Fifteen minutes later I became a member and went home feeling happy that after all the war years I was going to play tennis again, something I had done almost daily in Indonesia before leaving for Holland. When I tried to buy a racket the next day I found that it was impossible to buy a new one, but I might be able to obtain one in a second-hand store or perhaps by placing an advertisement in the newspaper. However, I was fortunate, the first sporting goods store I visited had several used rackets for sale and I bought one inexpensively.

Towards the end of July I received an invitation to attend the parade in Den Bosch on August third where I was to be presented with the Bronze Lion by Queen Wilhelmina. Of course, I asked Anna if she would like to come too. At the end of July I moved into my new digs and that same day asked Anna if she would be interested in joining the tennis club, not knowing that she was a keen tennis player and, like me, had not played for quite a while. She agreed to go with me the next time and also join the club; she even had her own racket! From this day on we saw each other almost daily and often going out for dinner, dancing, or to see a movie. There were no declarations of love; it seemed that we felt that we belonged to each other and simply enjoyed each other's company.

On the third of August I put on my uniform for the parade. Hank had received a similar invitation and he and Auda picked up Anna and me and we drove to Den Bosch. When we arrived at the parade grounds, there were masses of spectators already there. There was a military band and about a hundred strong military honour guard. Hank and I were directed to where we should line up to await the arrival of the Queen who arrived accompanied by Prince Bernhard and her entourage. The band struck up the national anthem and the Queen and the Prince walked over to where we were lined up and standing at attention.

The Queen walked down the line and presented each person with a medal, the first four received the Military Willems Order[14], followed by presentations of the Bronze Lion to each of the recipients. Then it was my turn. The Queen stood in front of me, looked me straight in the eyes and said: 'I am so glad to see you here!' and then pinned the medal (the Order of the Bronze Lion) on my chest and shook hands. My heart swelled with pride; she had recognized me and remembered our thirty-minute conversation more than three years ago! Prince Bernhard came over and congratulated me on receiving my medal and said that he was glad that I had made it through safely.

The presentations completed, the band started playing again almost drowning out the applause of the

---

spectators. The honour guard paraded past us and that was the end of the ceremony, although we all lingered to chat with our colleagues whom we had not seen for a long time.

Chapter Eighteen

Proposing to Anna, Receiving the M.C., Getting Married

Anna asked me if I would like to go to Brielle one weekend to meet her parents. Brielle is one of the oldest cities in Holland dating back to before the fifteenth century; I had never been there and wanted to meet Anna's parents so I readily agreed. We had both entered in a tennis tournament that was to be played over two weekends but, since we did not expect to survive to play in the second weekend, Anna called her parents to ask them if she could come home that weekend with a friend.

However, although Anna was eliminated in the third round, I, quite unexpectedly, made it to the finals. So Anna went home by herself, by train and a ferry to Brielle. She was met by her parents at the dock who were quite surprised that she was alone. Anna explained that I had not been able to come because I had to play in the final of the tennis tournament. Tennis players would understand this but her Dad was not impressed; if I thought it more important to play tennis than to meet her parents then our relationship was probably not very serious. To make matters worse, I lost my match and spent the rest of the weekend hanging around the club. I really missed Anna's company and decided, then and there, that this was the girl I wanted to spend the rest of my life with. On Sunday evening there was a knock on my door; it was Anna and of course, I invited her in. We looked at each other, we kissed, and I asked her to marry me. She nodded and said 'yes!' Then we kissed some more and enjoyed each other's company for the rest of the evening. We listened to 'Midnight in Munich,' an American radio station that was mostly broadcasting popular wartime songs. Anna told me that her mother was a little disappointed that I had not come with her but that her father was annoyed that I had stayed to play tennis! It was the beginning of September, and my birthday was on the twentieth, a Friday. We decided to go to Brielle the day after my birthday so that I could meet her parents. My daily activities had changed so drastically during the last few months that the war was almost forgotten. Anna had seen me in uniform a few times so she knew that I had been involved in the war but had no clue about my war experiences. I had never talked about it, she had never asked, and neither did her parents when we visited them.

The day after my birthday came and Anna and I were on our way to Brielle. I had never been to that part of Holland and enjoyed the short ferry trip across the water. The ferry docked right in town and Anna's parents were there to welcome us. As soon as we reached their house Anna told her parents that I had proposed and she had accepted, but we decided that this was the day that we were formally engaged, September 21, 1946. Anna took me on a tour of the city with its many old, historic features; a very interesting city indeed with remnants of the old wall, the moat, and draw bridges. Anna had quite a few relatives living in, and close to Brielle, and I probably met most of them that weekend. We returned to The Hague the next day and the following weeks were spent working and, if it was not raining, playing tennis.

A few days later I learned that my mother was on her way to Holland. Oddly enough she was on the same boat that my sister and I were on just a few months earlier. By this time, after a few months on my new job I had started to enjoy my work a bit more. It had become almost a certainty that I would be sent overseas; I was told that I would be going to Dutch New Guinea, probably within a few months! My stay in New Guinea would be for a period of three years. I was given some literature with information of what to take and what I would need to know about working there. There was a section pertaining to married employees that said 'wives' would probably follow six to eight months later, as soon as accommodation was available. As soon as I saw Anna I gave her the news and told her that if we were not married before I left we would not see each other for three years.

Of course we decided we needed to get married as soon as possible and that we must tell her parents. We went to the phone in the hall and called; her dad answered the phone. I gave him my news and told him that we had decided to get married right away. There was a moment of silence at the other end and then: 'Well, if that is what you both want to do, you'd better get married' and he then called Anna's mother to the phone. I handed the phone to Anna who gave her mother the big news. Her mother seemed to be more enthusiastic than her dad who, I suspect, would have liked a more formal engagement and marriage. After all, I had not even asked him if I could marry Anna!

When my mother arrived in Holland we told her the news and she was delighted. Our first task, which was quickly accomplished, was to find and rent a furnished two-room apartment on the ground floor close to where Anna worked. We served notice to our landlady that we would vacate our rooms by December fifteenth.

The British Ambassador to the Netherlands, Sir Neville Bland, had invited us to a luncheon at the embassy on December thirteenth, the day before our wedding. It was a delightful occasion. The First Secretary took us to the embassy where we met the Ambassador and Lady Bland. After cocktails and lunch, the ambassador read the recommendation accompanying the presentation of the award to me of the Military Cross, after which the nine-year old daughter of Sir and Lady Bland presented Anna with a bouquet of flowers. The lovely little girl curtsied for Anna as she gave her the flowers. Anna had told them during the luncheon that we were to be married the next day and on our way out, the First Secretary took us into his office, opened a drawer of his desk, and took out four bottles of liquor and gave them to us. 'This is for the celebration after the wedding,' he said. It was a very welcome gift as liquor by the bottle was still not available. Then, Anna and I parted ways and I went to my mother's apartment.

We were married the next day and had the wedding dinner afterwards in a large, swanky restaurant in The Hague. After the dinner we went to the train station and boarded the train to the picturesque town of Amersfoort for our honeymoon. I remember very little of our honeymoon, except for the fact that it had turned bitterly cold and, unable to get a taxi to our hotel, we had to walk to the hotel which was some way outside the city, into a bitterly cold north easterly wind. At the hotel there were a lot of soldiers who, according to the clerk at the desk, were apparently temporarily stationed there while doing exercises close by. Only the lounge was heated all the time and the dining room only at mealtimes. No other rooms were heated because of a shortage of coal. So for the week of our honeymoon we had to make the best of it spending most of the days either in stores or watching a matinee show in town, and the evenings in the heated lounge of the hotel until it was time to go to bed.

A week later we were back in The Hague, in our apartment. The weather was still very cold but the building had central heating and was nice and warm. Christmas came and New Year's Day and I still had not heard when I was going overseas. When I went to the personnel office to ask about the delay, I was told that the problem was getting a seat on the plane. They offered me the alternative of going by ship, which was exactly what I wanted! I was immediately booked to leave on the M.V. Oranje leaving at the end of January. I had no idea that this was the reason for the delay and happy that I now had a firm date and that I would be going by ship instead of by plane. I knew that the M.V. Oranje was relatively new, built shortly before the war, because I had read a news item just after its maiden voyage to the East Indies. The ship was designed to reduce the fees for passing through the Suez Canal that were based on the area of the ship measured at the waterline. The ship was wide at the bottom, narrow at the waterline and wide above again. This succeeded in reducing the fees but its shape made the ship susceptible to severe sideways rocking, so severe that wings had to be installed on both sides.

January sped by and the Shell Company gave me the last two weeks off to prepare for my departure.

On the day of my departure Anna and I travelled to Amsterdam where the 'Oranje' was docked. Anna's parents and my mother joined us on board for a farewell drink in the lounge. When the intercom announced that all visitors had to leave the ship, I said goodbye to our parents, but Anna stayed till the last call came and we had to say goodbye. All passengers were on deck waving goodbye to their loved ones on shore, but soon they were out of sight. It was the end of January, 1947.

Chapter Nineteen

Three Years in New Guinea: 1947-1950

So, my journey to Jakarta began; a voyage that took about a month and was very enjoyable and I was pleased to be going by boat rather than by air. Even as we sailed through the Gulf of Biscay, notorious for bad storms, the weather was delightful with light winds. However, there had been a storm a few days earlier causing a big swell and the ship to rock violently. We reached the swell some time during the night and by the morning I had to hang on to anything available in order to reach the bathroom and the only way I could dress was to either sit or lie down. I recalled the story about installing wings to the hull to counteract the rocking and decided that they were not having much effect.

There was only one other person in the dining room for breakfast, so I joined him. As I did so there was a tremendous crash and dishes came spilling out of the cupboards and clattering on the floor. Then a big fire extinguisher bouncing down the stairs; when it had reached the bottom it suddenly released a white column of powder coating everything in the dining room. At this point we made for the stairs and out onto the deck into the fresh air.

I spent most of the day in a deck chair reading and enjoying the winter sun as walking on deck was next to impossible. A few others, obviously seasick, came on deck later on. I suspect they were giving the personnel a chance to clean their cabins. I had lunch and dinner in solitary splendour, feeling fortunate that I was not, and never had been, seasick.

The next morning was calm and I looked out to see land close by; we were about to enter the Strait of Gibraltar. Later, as we sailed through the Mediterranean I remembered that, before I had got the position with Shell, I had answered an advertisement in the paper for crewmen to sail around the world in a sixteen meter steel yacht. I had received a letter thanking me for my application and although they now had a full crew, there might be a cancellation. About six weeks later I heard on the news that a Dutch yacht had been shipwrecked in a violent storm in the Mediterranean and had washed up on the coast of Egypt. The crew survived and were in Egypt awaiting their return to Holland. How different my path would have been had I been selected! I had sailed through the Mediterranean on two other voyages and found it hard to believe that there could ever be storms. On this my third visit there once again it was beautiful sunny weather, with very calm seas. Our ship anchored in Colombo for several hours that brought back many memories. It had been less than a year since I was last there.

On my arrival in Jakarta, I took a cab to the hotel where my dad was the manager. He was expecting me and delighted when I stepped into his office. It was great to see him again after so many years and we talked a lot during the next few days. He had lost a lot of weight after his experience during the war years but looked well and seemed happy. He had luxurious quarters in the hotel and I was able to stay there. I had reported my arrival to the Shell office that was making arrangements to fly me to New Guinea in a few days.

Three days later my plane left in the early morning for New Guinea. It was a long, tedious flight and very uncomfortable. The plane was a Dakota or DC3, termed the workhorse of the Second World War. The seats were long wooden benches along the sides and our luggage was piled in the centre. We made one stop at the east end of the island of Java, at Surabaya where I was born and where most of the passengers got off. The remaining three of us were all Shell employees destined for New Guinea. The plane flew on to Biak, a small island north of New Guinea, a former US airbase during WW2. The airbase was an extraordinary sight with literally hundreds of airplanes on both sides of the runway, left there by the US army. There were three planes on the tarmac and one small building close to where our plane had come to a stop. A lone person was behind a counter inside this air-conditioned building who told us that a Shell plane would be picking us up in a few hours and to make ourselves comfortable. I wondered where the people were from the other three planes, when two people walked in carrying a huge box of parts. They sat down and proceeded to take the parts out one by one making a list of the part numbers; I concluded from their accents that they were Americans. They then took one of the many catalogues of parts from the counter and proceeded to check the price for each part. Finally, this list was given to the 'station manager' who totalled the numbers, divided the total by five and gave them an invoice in US dollars which they promptly paid in cash. The Americans loaded the parts onto their plane and took off.

I must have looked puzzled to the Chinese person behind the desk. He explained that he had purchased the entire stock of former US warplanes on the island and was now selling off the parts. He told me: 'The buyers come here, strip the parts they want from the planes, pay me in cash and leave. I have some ladders they can borrow and they all bring their own tools. Every other week my brother flies in from Hong Kong to take over from me so that I can take off to buy food and supplies. He likes doing this because I let him keep the money he collects for the parts he sells!' I surmised that he probably deposited a suitcase full of cash in the bank on each trip too! What an incredibly simple and lucrative business. He added that he knew nothing about airplane parts and just accepted the word of the buyers.

The three of us decided to have a look in the planes while we were waiting for our flight to see if we could find anything usable, perhaps some instruments. The only tool we had was a pocket screwdriver so if we did find something we would probably have had a hard time removing it. However, we found nothing and it was boiling hot inside the planes in the tropical sun, so we soon decided to retreat to the nice, cool building.

Our plane, a Catalina, arrived after about an hour and during that time the people that landed before us came in with a load of parts, paid and left. Two other planes had arrived by now to find and buy needed parts.

We flew to the island of Morotai, another former US airbase, now used by Shell as the staging centre for their operations on New Guinea. The US army had left all the buildings intact and these were now being used by Shell. I was assigned to a Quonset hut, situated right on the beach, sharing with three other employees. This was to be my home for the next four months while they were building the bases at Sorong, about 450 kilometres to the southeast and also at Steenkool, another 300 kilometres further east, both on mainland New Guinea. Our salaries were kept in our accounts at the head office in The Hague. We had no need of money because the Shell provided everything free, even cigarettes and liquor. There were no stores on the island.

Four months later I was transferred to Sorong where I was again assigned a Quonset hut sharing with three others who had arrived from Morotai before me. Some of the older employees were already living in houses and they were either already reunited with their wives or were waiting for them en route from Holland. It was Shell's policy to have the wives come out as soon as possible and it was easy to understand their policy. Wives changed the atmosphere in the camp right away; men without wives tended to congregate every night to drink and play poker and sometimes get rowdy. Once their wives had arrived most of them spent the evenings together or with other couples playing bridge, or listening to music from ancient record players, the kind you had to wind after every record. There was no radio other than short wave and that had rather poor reception.

Two months later I was transferred to Steenkool about twenty kilometres inland, located by a very winding river. As the river had no straight stretch long enough for the Shell plane, a Catalina, to land, we were dropped off at the mouth of the river and picked up by a small motorboat that carried passengers and freight up the river. We passed through mangroves and as it was high tide all we could see were trees sticking out of the water and no land. In fact there was a tidal range of about twenty feet, sometimes more as far inland as the camp and quite a distance beyond. The result was that the river would flow to the ocean for about fourteen hours a day and inland the rest of the time. It took a few months for me to get used to 'water flowing upstream!' The camp was situated on high land east of the river. I had been told in Sorong that I was to get a house in Steenkool and that arrangements had been made to have Anna come out on the next available ship. It was now more than seven months since I left Holland. I had been assigned a houseboy, 'Urias', a friendly native Papuan.

Anna finally arrived at the end of November, not by Catalina and motorboat but by MTB (Motor Torpedo Boat) that Shell had recently acquired. She came with all her luggage and a big trunk full of 'stuff' that I had left behind, including an American Jungle Carbine and three German Luger pistols. Anna told me later that the trunk was packed in the presence of a Customs employee and that her mother had managed to pack the weapons and ammunition in the trunk right under his nose. When it was full, it was locked and sealed by the customs man who gave her a signed declaration that it had been inspected and did not contain any illegal or declarable goods!

I was surprised and pleased that she had brought these items for I had totally forgotten about them. I even thought that I might do some boar hunting later. However, hunting was almost impossible because of the steep terrain and the impenetrable jungle. One native in the camp who was an experienced hunter offered to hunt boar for us. As we hardly ever had fresh meat, his offer was appealing. At first we took his offer with a grain of salt but when he came in with one and occasionally two boars he turned us into believers. I asked him one day what type of gun he was using, his reply was that he used a bow and arrow! When I offered him my carbine he shook his head saying he would sooner use the bow and arrow because a gun makes too much noise scaring away other boars.

Our house was built on a concrete slab and made of woven bamboo on a wood frame with a thatched roof. It had a bedroom at one end, a living room at the other, and between them a veranda, behind which was a bathroom with a toilet and a tiny kitchen, just big enough to make a pot of tea or coffee and to put our dirty dishes. Our meals were prepared in the kitchen of the recreation building and we could either eat there or have them delivered to our house. The food was generally fairly good but Anna, as a vegetarian, was quite a challenge for the cook.

My job could best be described as a 'Jack of all trades.' I was responsible for the native payroll, in charge of native personnel, who numbered about two hundred when I arrived but grew to more than two thousand two years later. Soon after my arrival I was also appointed as the liaison between the Shell and the personnel of McGraw & Co., a big New York construction firm, contracted to clear the roadway and build a road between our camp and our first drilling site ten miles further inland into the hills. McGraw & Co. had submitted their bid on the basis of a fly-over of the terrain assuming the conditions below the green crowns would be the same as conditions in North America. They were surprised to find six-foot diameter ironwood trees instead, which had to be felled by digging around the base of the tree and placing several dynamite charges around it. The contract had to be changed to a cost plus basis.

New Guinea was home to many exotic birds, about three thousand species of large orchids and eight thousand small species of orchids. An area in the camp had been set aside for a tennis court but building a court had a very low priority, so I decided to build a clay court in my spare time with the help of Dick Hebbert, an Englishman, who came to Steenkool about six months after me. Dick was also a keen tennis player and when I approached him about building a court he was very willing to help.

About three months after Anna arrived she announced that she was pregnant! The fact that there was no doctor in Steenkool had never occurred to us. When Anna was in her seventh month I talked to the doctor in Sorong on short wave radio and asked him if he wanted to see her. On learning that Anna had arrived in Steenkool in early November, he told me to call him in early July and he would then make arrangements to have her flown to Sorong. So in July, as planned, we traveled by motorboat to the mouth of the river and we sitting on the boxes that were going to be loaded on the Catalina. Anna was able to stay with friends in Sorong and a week later I had a call over the radio to inform me that she had delivered a healthy baby boy! It was the 27th of July, 1948, exactly nine months to the day that Anna arrived in Steenkool!
Two days later an elated new father flew to Sorong, accompanied by our dog Rex, an Irish Setter that we had somehow acquired since Anna had arrived. I was only able to stay for a few days but Anna was in Sorong for another week before returning home. It is amazing that Anna never saw a doctor till about a

week before she gave birth, and she made those long trips in the open motorboat to the mouth of the river and back in the tropical sun without thinking it was unusual!

The tennis court was not even close to being finished. The ground was fairly level but there were still many pieces of root sticking out which had to be pulled out by hand. Every time we raked the ground we seemed to end up with as many pieces as we had the time before; it was a very tedious and seemingly never ending job. However we had acquired a motor roller and rolled the court, back and forth, back and forth until finally we had it in an acceptable shape for play. We ordered the poles and the net and installed them. It felt so good to be able to hit the ball again and we spent many hours after work and on weekends playing tennis, or I should say hitting the ball back and forth because we had no lines and the court was wide open on all sides. We could only play in the early morning or late afternoon; it was far too hot during the day. There were only the three of us so we took turns; the one that was not playing having to retrieve the balls that had gone off the court.

At the beginning of 1949 we went on a three-week all-expenses paid holiday to Sidney, Australia, compliments of the Shell. A very welcome break indeed! The Catalina flew us to Darwin where we were to board a DC3 the next day to fly us to Sidney. But when the authorities checked our papers they saw that Paul, our son had not had a smallpox vaccination. He would have to have one and we would have to stay in Darwin until there was evidence that the vaccine had taken. Fortunately two days later they were satisfied that it had and we could fly on.

The trip took us across the Australian desert, over the Blue Mountains into Sidney. We left Darwin early in the morning and as the day wore on, the heat of the sun created huge air pockets causing the plane to sometimes drop a few hundred feet. Paul was in a basket on the floor in front of us and became sick, as did many other passengers. We made a refuelling stop at Alice Springs. All I can remember was the horrendous heat and hundreds of flies that seemed to be determined to land on our faces while we waited at the little terminal. Desert surrounded us and in the distance we could see the city. It was hot in New Guinea, but nothing in comparison to Alice Springs. The humidity was very low and although I could feel the perspiration pouring out of my body, my clothes stayed relatively dry. It was twilight as we flew over the mountains and in the distance we could see the lights of Sidney. The first time in almost two years that we saw city lights!

We spent the days shopping and the evenings window shopping or going to a movie. Baby Paul was with us of course and we could leave him in the crib in our hotel room as the hotel provided a baby-sitting service. Every morning there was not enough pressure to take water to the fifth floor where we were staying; we had to leave the taps open till the water started flowing. One morning we opened the tap and as usual there was no water and unfortunately we left our room without turning the tap off. We were only away for a very short while but when we came back a very angry hotel manager greeted us. While we were away, the hot water tap had started to run filling the room with steam. It had overflowed the basin onto the floor of the room and was leaking into the room below.

One night we went to the concert hall to listen to a piano recital by a well-known Canadian pianist. It was in a very old building and we could hear the passing streetcars. Then, halfway through the performance it started to rain and the noise of the rain on the corrugated metal roof almost drowned out the music. The magnificent Sidney Opera House built on the water close to the Sidney Harbour Bridge later replaced this concert hall. We spent a week in Sidney and then traveled by train into the Blue Mountains where we stayed at the Lapstone Hotel for the rest of our vacation. It was a luxurious resort with tennis courts, a golf course, and a swimming pool; during the war it had been reserved for American army officers on holidays.

While staying in Sydney Anna found an exclusive ladies dress shop. It was considered exclusive because the lady that owned the store assured Anna that all her dresses were one of a kind. How surprised we were to find that, at the next big party in New Guinea, several other ladies had the same dresses all bought at that 'exclusive' ladies dress shop. The men found it hilarious but the ladies were not amused!

Our holiday over, one evening there was suddenly a loud roar from the native quarters followed by gunshots. Knowing this meant trouble, I grabbed a flashlight and as I was heading out of the door to go to the native camp, a couple of the other employees joined me, both armed with rifles. They had orders from the boss that we were to go together to the camp armed with rifles. I told them to tell the boss I was going to the camp unarmed and alone.

There was a contingent of six Ambonese soldiers stationed at the native camp and I knew the shots had come from there; I was hoping that no one was hurt. I approached the camp, shining my flashlight on my face now and then, to let them know that it was me; the noise grew louder and louder. The source of the racket came from the natives who were gathered in one corner of the camp. I jumped on a table, shone the light on my face and screamed 'Quiet!' at the top of my lungs.

Suddenly it was dead quiet. I asked if someone could tell me what was going on, and they all started shouting again, so I yelled 'Quiet' again. In the silence that followed I asked for just one of them and only one to come and tell me what was going on. I looked around and finally somebody spoke up and said that someone had seen a ghost! 'I want that person to come here and tell me what he saw!' Nobody came.

I waited a few moments and then told them to go back to their own quarters and to make no more noise. They obeyed and all left quietly. I stayed for a while to talk to the person who had told me about the ghost. It had all started upon completion of the new jetty that was built at the river; this should have been followed by a ceremony to appease the ghosts and when this did not happen they had grown increasingly excited. When somebody thought that he saw a ghost they thought that they were in for it. I told him to go around all the quarters and tell them that the ceremony would be held the next day.

When I got back to my own camp all the employees were waiting for me, including the boss, the Americans and the two Canadian drillers. I told them what had happened and assured them that there would be no further trouble. A few of the employees stayed on; they had obviously been drinking and seemed to be disappointed that all the excitement was over. Then we saw people coming down the path from the native camp and when they came close we saw two Ambonese soldiers, apparently wanting to explain why they had fired a few shots. Suddenly, one of the employees tore the rifle away from one of the soldiers with the intention of killing him. I grabbed the gun away from him, gave it back to the soldier and asked one of the Canadians to take the troublemaker home.

The Canadian I asked was Shortie Hawkins; soon after he arrived in Steenkool we had become great friends and he was always telling me that I should go to Canada.

Shortly after this incident I was transferred back to Sorong where we got a house right on the ocean with our own fruit trees, two banana and two papaya trees. The people who had moved out asked us if we would mind if their cat stayed with us until her kittens were born. We had never had cats and were not very enthusiastic about the idea, but we finally agreed after they assured us that they would come to take mother and kittens away as soon as they were old enough to be moved. We had also wondered how our dog would react to the presence of a cat, but Rex and the cat hit it off right away and were soon sleeping cuddled up against each other. When the kittens arrived Rex would often lick them and later on play with them, ever so gently first but later not quite so gently, but never hurting them. The owners of the cat returned as promised, and we begged them to leave us two kittens, to which they readily agreed. Our three animals gave us many hours of laughter just watching them play. When we took the dog out for a walk, the cats always came along running and cavorting all around us. When they saw another dog, they would always go underneath Rex where they would stay till the stranger was at a safe distance.

Sorong, had by now become quite a large community. There was a large office building, a hospital, a recreation hall with a large dining area, and two tennis courts. Life in Sorong turned out to be considerably more eventful than it had been in Steenkool. The Shell Company had three six meter sailboats that we could take out on weekends as long as we could convince them that we had sailing experience. The waters around Sorong contained many coral islands and also coral reefs just below the surface that made sailing through these waters quite treacherous. One of the crew always had to stand on the bow watching out for a sudden change in the colour of the water, a sure sign of a reef below the surface. A quick 180-degree turn was the only way to avoid hitting a reef in this area. When you looked down into the water you would see all kinds of beautifully coloured fish, making our sailing trips very enjoyable.

Early evening we could watch the native fishermen going into the water with a torch in one hand and a spear in the other. We discovered that they were after huge lobsters; one lobster was enough for a family meal. Occasionally I managed to intercept a fisherman as he left and buy the lobster from him....for about fifty cents! We had to borrow a huge pot to cook them, half filling it with ocean water and bringing the water to a boil outside on a kerosene burner. When the water boiled, I would give Anna the lid with the instruction to slam the lid down on the pot as soon as I had thrown the lobster in the pot. I would then grab the handle of the lid and hold it down as hard as possible until all the commotion in the pot had died down. They were simply delicious and provided us with many days of gastronomic delight. One day a directive was issued by head office that we were required to organize an armed group of people with a military background in order to be able to defend ourselves in the case of an uprising. The head of personnel had been a army major so he became the commanding officer and I became second in command. We were issued with rifles that were kept under lock and key in the office. The fact that I was second-in-command did not sit very well with the older employees of the group, but there was nothing that they could do about it. I was amused that I was in charge of so many of the big bosses, but I tried to handle it as tactfully as possible and avoided rubbing it in too much despite wanting to do so at times. Most of the gatherings ended with all of us heading for the recreation hall for a few beers.

When my three-year contract ended we left to return to Holland. We left Rex and the two cats in the care of friends who were moving into our house after we left. Our friends from Zandvoort, Auda and Hank, were now living in Bangkok, where Hank was an agent for KLM Royal Dutch Airlines; Anna had kept in touch with Auda ever since Zandvoort. They invited us to stay with them in Bangkok on our way to Holland and we readily accepted. We stayed in their house just outside Bangkok for about a week before returning to Holland. We went sightseeing every day finding Bangkok a very interesting and beautiful city; the people were very friendly and helpful. We visited a Buddhist temple one day and like everybody else took off our shoes and socks, leaving them outside the temple before going inside and kneeling down. Nobody paid the slightest attention to us and we sat through a whole service before leaving.

When we arrived in Bangkok the immigration officer told us that he would be keeping our passports and be returning them to us as we left. I felt uneasy about handing over our only identification but Hank assured us that this was usual and that he would see that they were returned to us. On the drive to his house he told us that most tourists were charged a sum of money that was pocketed by the immigration officer himself, but Hank had told him that if he ever did this to any of the KLM passengers he would report him to his superiors. One soon learns how to deal with corruption when working in these countries! Our passports were returned without any trouble and two days later we arrived in Holland where we were welcomed by Anna's parents and sister, and my sister who were seeing our son Paul for the first time.

Two and a half years in New Guinea had taken a toll on Anna who had lost quite a bit of weight. I have to admit that this had escaped me entirely because she never complained except about the heat. A few days after we arrived in Holland she told me that she would rather not go back to New Guinea. I was happy to agree because the natives had been a problem during the last six months of my term. I could feel the tension and certainly understand that they wanted their freedom and independence. I had fought in the war to gain our freedom and could certainly understand these people; the Dutch had ruled them for almost five centuries! They had prospered during that time and had certainly not been mistreated, at least not to my knowledge. When I was a child, growing up at home, we always treated them with respect and when my dad took early retirement and left the plantation, all his employees were standing there saying good-bye to us and all had tears in their eyes.

Having made this decision I went to see the personnel manager to tell him that I would prefer not go back to the East Indies and asked to be sent to the West Indies instead. He flatly refused my request on the grounds that I spoke the language of the east and not of the west. So I decided to try to get a visa for Canada; I would go there during my holidays and if I liked it, to stay there and submit my resignation to Shell. When I told the personnel manager of my intentions, he became angry would not believe that I would be able to find a job in Canada in such a short time. I replied that I did not know if I could either but if I did, he would get my resignation.

I went to the Canadian Consulate to ask them what I needed to get a visa. First, I was told I needed a letter from a Canadian citizen who would be willing to sponsor me. Once this letter was received, it would probably take several weeks, and even months, before I would get a visa. I explained that I wanted to visit Canada before the end of my furlough from my company about two months later. After some deliberation it was suggested that if I could produce a letter that said that it was desirable that I be in Canada for some reason, it might be possible to give me a visitor's visa which I could then convert into a permanent one in Canada.

So I wrote to my Canadian friend Shorty Hawkins to tell him what I needed to be able to go to Canada. Within ten days I received a word from Shorty with a letter saying that he was prepared to sponsor me and another letter from the owner of the company he worked for that said more or less that my presence in Canada was very desirable, as otherwise there would be bad consequences for the oil industry! I handed these letters to the immigration officer at the consulate, who told me that I would probably have my visa within a week. Years later I learned that entering Canada with a visitor's visa and then applying for a permanent one was highly illegal. But I was the innocent party because that is what the immigration officer suggested I should do. Also, years later, I was sponsoring somebody who wanted to immigrate to Canada and while talking to an immigration officer in Edmonton, he told me that my case was always used at the school for future immigration officers as an example of how not to do it. He never expected that he would ever meet me in person. A week later with my visa in hand, I boarded a plane for Canada. It was May, 1950.

POSTSCRIPT – A new life in Canada

I arrived in Montreal with two hundred dollars, one hundred of which I had bought on the black market. I traveled by train to Calgary for two days totally absorbed by the immense landscape going by and determining that Canada was the country where I wanted to spend the rest of my life. Shorty was at the station in Calgary to pick me up. I had one dollar left in my pocket! He told me that he was the tool pusher of a drilling rig and that he could get me a job as a roughneck. It wasn't exactly what I expected but I had to have a job. In fact, I earned good money and quickly realized how fortunate I was.

Then the Korean War broke out and memories of being parted from my parents and sister during the Second World War hastened our decision that Anna and our son should come as soon as possible. She arrived in Montreal during a railway strike and was stranded for a week in one room of a boarding house on the top floor, a room with only a skylight and no windows, before she could travel by train to join me.

By now I needed a car to get to the drilling rigs. I found a 1930 Model 'A' Ford two-seater for $90 in a junkyard that actually started after putting in some oil and gas. Since it had no windows and only a manifold heater I fitted myself out from an Army Surplus catalogue with leather, sheepskin lined helmet, jacket, pants and boots for of less than $40; but I still often came home stone cold. The car never let me down and always started, sometimes with the help of a 'smudge pot', an old paint can with a rag soaked in used oil. I would light the rag and place the can underneath the engine block and wait to hear the pop of the gas in the carburetor igniting before starting the engine!

On February 17, 1951 our second son Menno was born. In April I was injured and we moved to a more suitable job in Calgary on June 17, 1951, arriving in a blinding snowstorm!

That same year I was transferred to Edmonton and we lived in there for the next twenty-three years, working in the oil industry. My wish for a girl to complete the family was fulfilled in July, 1953 when our daughter Marilyn was born.

In 1960, I became production manager for the Gulf Oil Co, and in 1966 I started my own consulting business relating to oil and gas well completions and testing the wells for deliverability. My major client was the Gulf Oil Co. who engaged me initially to do most of their 'tight hole' completions and later on to do their well completions in the arctic.

Wherever I went I always had my fishing gear in my car, and there was usually a stream nearby with rainbow trout or grayling; I got to know most of the good fishing spots in western Alberta. My son Paul became a very keen fisherman and when school was out I would often take him along. Menno sometimes came but he was more interested in golfing or working on his car.

We moved to Victoria, British Columbia in 1974 and in 1975 I retired from consulting.

I bought a vintage 1950 twenty-four foot boat with a hull of cedar planking over oak ribs and a four-cylinder gas engine that was even older than the boat. Fishing in the Saanich Inlet was very good and catching the limit was usually assured. I probably spent as many happy hours repairing and painting the boat as I did fishing!

Dogs have always played a big role in our lives and still do. We have enjoyed them all immensely. Anna and I always seem to keep busy during our retirement years and I often wonder how I ever had the time to work.

And today, in good health, with a loving wife, three children, all happily married and five grandchildren, I am a happy man.

RECOMMENDATION FOR AN AWARD OF THE MILITARY CROSS
2/Lieut. Leonard George MULHOLLAND
Pers. No 4405
Royal Netherlands Armed Forces[15]

2/Lieut. Leonard George MULHOLLAND, of the Royal Netherlands Armed Forces, arrived in this country on the 11th February 1944, after having escaped from HOLLAND by way of Sweden.

On arrival here he volunteered to return to HOLLAND to carry out a mission. He received special training and on the night of the 5th/6th of July 1944 he was dropped by parachute in that country together with two other members of his team.

His mission was to try to contact any underground organizations which he might consider not to have been penetrated and to reorganize these elements into an active force; to arrange to receive arms by air and to maintain W/T contact with the U.K.

He contacted the underground organizations and re-organized the active units into a potential fighting force, arranged their reception committees and generally raised their morale, which was on the wane owing to heavy enemy activity.

Through his operator he sent valuable information on German activities, intentions in the port of Rotterdam and troop movements. He asked for special material to sink certain blockade ships that the

---

[15] The Military Cross and the citation read to me by the British Ambassador to the Netherlands, Sir Neville Bland, in the presence of Lady Bland, Anna Knape and the First Secretary during a private luncheon at the British Embassy in The Hague on December 13, 1946, the day before we were to be married.

Germans intended to put the port out of action. Explosives were sent to him and he arranged the sinking of three large vessels at their mooring berths.

He sent information on rocket sites in HOLLAND, as a result of which it has been possible to take counter action.

On SHAEF's instructions he and his organization cut the main railway routes being used by the Germans and, in conjunction with the airborn operation in HOLLAND, sent forward couriers with valuable intelligence information.

2/Lieut. MULHOLLAND is still in the field, valiantly carrying out his mission in spite of the hazardous nature of his work.

8 Juni 1946

No. 34

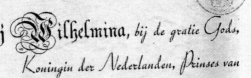

Wij Wilhelmina, bij de gratie Gods,

Koningin der Nederlanden, Prinses van

Oranje—Nassau, enz., enz., enz.

Op de voordracht van Onzen Minister van Oorlog:
d.d. 29 Mei 1946, Geheim Litt. K 103;

HEBBEN GOEDGEVONDEN EN VERSTAAN:

Toe te kennen den BRONZEN LEEUW aan:
den, als zoodanig tijdelijk benoemden,
Reserve-kapitein voor algemeenen dienst,
L. G. MULHOLLAND,

wegens:

"Bij de uitvoering van zeer belangrijke opdrachten in bezet
Nederlandsch gebied, zich onderscheiden door bijzonder moedig
en voortvarend optreden. Daarbij herhaaldelijk blijk gegeven
van groot doorzettingsvermogen en initiatief, en alle gevaren
ten spijt, zich steeds met groote zelfopoffering gewijd aan
het dienen van de Nederlandsche Zaak."

Onze Minister enz.

Het Loo , den   8 Juni   1946

(get.) WILHELMINA.

De Minister van Oorlog,

(get.) J.MEIJNEN

Overeenkomstig het oorspronkelijke,
De Secretaris-Generaal van het Ministerie van Oorlog,

(get.)   RIETVELD

Uitgegeven voor woordelijk gelijkluidend uittreksel,
De Secretaris-Generaal,

No. 2626
1324 - 146

**Proclamation by H.M. Queen Wilhelmina of the awarding of
The Order of the Bronze Lion to Captain L.G. Mulholland**

ONE TIME PAD CODE

We were issued about a dozen small sheets of paper on each of which were printed lines of random letters in five-letter groups, e.g., FKROM GWMVA KLENM and so on, each five-letter group being unique. Also, we were given a piece of silk, on which was a printed a table consisting of a top row with the letters A to Z, and below each top-row letter a column of letters A to Z, as shown in Fig. 1 and 2. Beside each upper case letter in the columns was a lower case letter, e.g., Qv, Uh, etc.

To encode a message, e.g., "Convoy left Rotterdam", the message would first be broken into five-letter groups as follows:

CONVO YLEFT ROTTE RDAMX.

That is, the message is broken into groups of five letters each. The X at the end is included to give a last group of five letters, four groups in total. Beneath the message were written six groups of five letters taken from the sheet of paper, one extra group in the beginning and one at the end as follows:

```
          C O NVO  YLEF T  ROTTE  RDAMX
    FKROM   GWMVA  KLENM  GHKLE  ROWLT  HRBGH
```
The whole sequence would then be:

```
1.           CO N VO  YLEF T  ROTTE  RDAMX
2.  FKROM  GWMVA  KLENM  GHKLE  ROWLT  HRBGH
3.           x e de g  xwh o y  t j r z h  i u y g w
4.  fqrmm   x e de g  xwh oy   t j r z h  I u y g w  hxbea
```

The extra first and last groups in 4 contained the security code. The security code, known to the receiving office in England might be "two plus six and four minus two". In the five-letter group FKROM, K is the second letter and, advancing (i.e., plus) six letters in the alphabet, gives q; O is the fourth letter and moving back (i.e., minus) two places gives m. Consequently, FKROM becomes fqrmm which becomes the first group of the coded message. Similarly, HRGBA becomes hxbea, and line(4) is then the coded message that was transmitted to the receiving office in London. While the German intelligence knew that the security code was in the first and last groups of a message, if an agent fell into enemy hands and was forced to send a message, he would simply change the security code so that the "friends across the water" would know that it came from the enemy.

To decode the message, the receiver would reverse the procedure described above. Once an agent had completed coding a message, He or she would cut from the sheet of paper the used five-letter groups - 6 groups in this case, 4 for the message and 2 for the security code – and destroy them. Each five-letter group was used only once, hence the name "One-Time Pad Code."

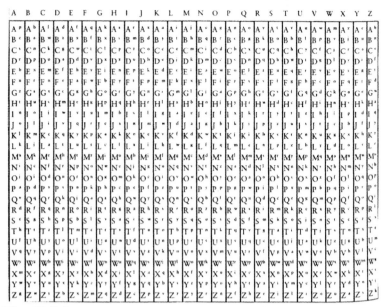

The 'Silk'

The actual 'Silk'

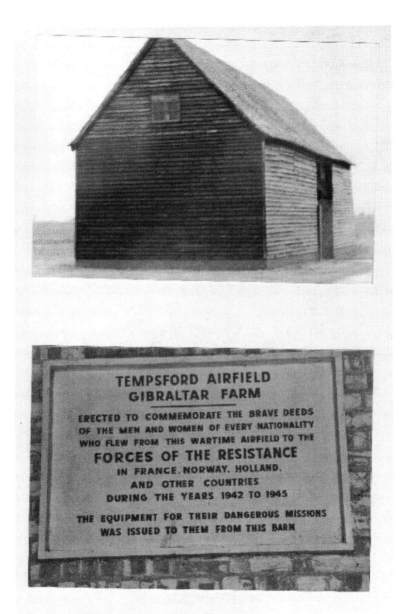

The 'Hut' at Tempsford Airfield in 2005, with commemorative plaque inside.

ISBN 141207320-0

9 781412 073202